HEALING
LIFE'S
HURTS

Make your anger work for you

GRAHAM BRETHERICK

MONARCH
BOOKS

Oxford, UK & Grand Rapids, Michigan, USA

First published in the UK in 2008 by Monarch Books
(a publishing imprint of Lion Hudson plc),
Wilkinson House, Jordan Hill Road, Oxford OX2 8DR.
Tel: +44 (0)1865 302750   Fax: +44 (0)1865 302757
Email: monarch@lionhudson.com
www.lionhudson.com

ISBN: 978-1-85424-874-9 (UK)
ISBN: 978-0-8254-6279-5 (USA)

Distributed by:
UK: Marston Book Services Ltd, PO Box 269, Abingdon, Oxon OX14 4YN;
USA: Kregel Publications, PO Box 2607, Grand Rapids, Michigan 49501

Unless otherwise stated, Scripture quotations are taken from the Holy
Bible, New International Version, © 1973, 1978, 1984 by the International
Bible Society. Used by permission of Hodder & Stoughton Ltd. All rights
reserved.

This book has been printed on paper and board independently certified as
having come from sustainable forests.

British Library Cataloguing Data
A catalogue record for this book is available from
the British Library.

Printed and bound in Wales by Creative Print & Design.

Contents

Acknowledgments

It is difficult (probably impossible) to give credit to everyone who has influenced me in the writing of this book. In my early years, I read considerably. I was always the student, looking to learn, because I realized that I was on a journey of discovery in my attempts to help others. Then came the day when I realized how much I needed help myself. That was when God brought Duane Harder, my pastor, back into my life. Over a six-year period, God used Duane to help me find real answers to the questions I had about my own life. In that process of re-learning, I began a study of the Scriptures that changed the way I approached learning. To a large degree I stopped reading other authors and began to ask the Holy Spirit to teach me from his Word. That is how this book came to be. However, I do want to acknowledge my thanks to all those authors and the people in my life who have had an impact on my overall thinking. But I especially want to acknowledge my deep gratitude to Duane and Marva Harder for their inestimable input into my life and writing. I do not know where I would be today without them.

I also have much to be thankful for in my church family, Northside Christian Fellowship of Lethbridge. Some of us have been together for thirty years, and in that journey we have shared together conflict, forgiveness and love many times. To my fellow elders, Mike Hastings, Doug Scales and Craig Webber – thank you for your faithfulness in working out differences, which has led to a development of character in me that would not have been possible without you. I am also grateful for the many close relationships with my fellow pastors in the 'Church of Lethbridge'. Our bond of unity has been made possible through forgiveness and reconciliation over many years.

I also want to acknowledge my gratefulness to my parents for their Godly input into the formative years of my life. I was privileged to grow up in a 'normal' home (whatever that is) and to benefit from being trained in Godly ways from my earliest days. To my parents, Ralph and Marjorie, I cannot say 'Thank you' enough times. You are receiving your reward in heaven.

My siblings, Judy, Grant, Ross, Lynne and Elaine, also contributed significantly to my development and learning. To them I also owe a debt of gratitude. To this day, when we get together (with their spouses and families), we still enjoy wonderful relationships and a bond of love that is the result of the love sown in our home by our parents. A special thanks to my twin brother, Grant, who has accepted me all my life and still believes in me to this day.

To my own family, I also wish to express the inexpressible. How can I thank you enough? Much of what I have learned in the crucible of life was formed in the daily family life that we have all shared together. So to Sam, Sarah, Andy, Nathan and Caleb – thank you for your love, patience, forgiveness and acceptance of an imperfect father working out his anger and forgiveness in our home.

To my wonderful and beautiful wife, Sherry, I cannot say enough. No one has taught me more about love and forgiveness than you. Today I am more in love with you than at any other point in our marriage. Sherry, you and I have learned all about anger and forgiveness together, and I want to publicly acknowledge how grateful I am to God for the life we share. So much of what I teach to others today has been learned in the day-to-day reality of our marriage. So to you, Sherry, I dedicate this book, and continually offer you my love and loyalty.

The person who has had the most significant influence in my life, without question, has been Jesus Christ. To truly understand forgiveness, one must be forgiven by God himself. To this end, Jesus came to live and die. And I have experienced his forgiveness countless times. My prayer is that every reader might also know the personal forgiveness of the God of the Universe, in the person of his Son, Jesus. May the Holy Spirit bring each of you the revelation of truth from God's Word and from this book.

Foreword

Through years of experience and a sensitivity to the work of the Holy Spirit, Graham Bretherick has been able to help others walk into new levels of freedom in Christ. This book is an expression of his life's message. His training in theology has helped him filter out the humanism from his postgraduate work in psychology and present a biblical alternative to the issues of the soul.

Our friendship with Graham goes back many years – in fact we considered him part of our family while he was doing summer work in an area where we were pastoring. His integrity, passion for truth and love of the Lord have made him a great asset to the church of Jesus Christ. Graham writes out of who he is.

Both my wife and I pray that as you read this book, you will find the One whose name is Counsellor and that, in finding him, you will be set free.

Duane Harder

Preface

The journey towards writing this book began several years ago. At an international church leaders' meeting in England in 1993, my wife Sherry and I were given a prophecy (a word of encouragement) by a man named Bryn Franklin. In this word to us, I was told that I would be given keys that would unlock certain doors. Bryn expressed it this way: 'I felt there were skills that God wanted to give you in the training and in the development in the area of counsel, in specific counsel, specialized counsel – that God would give you some keys in that area.'

Shortly after that conference, returning to work as a psychologist at Crossroads Counselling Centre in Lethbridge, I remember being challenged to look for real answers to the issues that my clients presented to me day after day. A principal concern was the way past hurts held people back from getting on with their present lives. Many people seemed captured by their bitterness. I needed real answers to see them set free. It was clear that I was dealing with a lot of buried anger in people, some of it buried for a long time. This anger directly affects how they solve present problems.

My spiritual director and pastor, Duane Harder, continually encouraged me to look in the Scriptures for answers to the problems and dilemmas I was facing. So, I began looking up the word 'anger' in its various forms in the Bible. After printing all the references from my computer concordance, I began examining the concept of anger in the Bible. This process revolutionized my thinking. God provides answers from the Bible to the personal problems we all face. His real answers could bring about real change in people's lives. Along with Sherry's daily intercession, I saw not only a remarkable difference in the counselling cases I was handling, but also a definite increase in successful outcomes.

One day, in a discussion with Dr Dick Dewert, President of The Miracle Channel in Lethbridge, I was asked to consider recording my anger workshop on videotape. As a result, *Healing Life's Hurts* was professionally developed and marketed through The Miracle Channel. As I continued to travel, conducting workshops as well as selling videotapes and DVDs, I was frequently asked for this material in book form. The Holy Spirit kept nudging me to listen to what was being asked of me, and so, with a sense that God wanted this material in print, I agreed to write a book. I trust God to use the material he gave me to help readers find greater freedom in Christ. This prayer is continually on my heart.

Introduction

Jim and Georgina were not getting along at all. (All the names and some of the circumstances mentioned in these stories and counselling references have been changed to protect the confidentiality of the clients I have counselled.) They were concerned, not only for their marriage, but for the effect their ongoing conflict had on their two children. They were leaders in the Christian community and, ironically, their calling was helping others with marriage problems. But with their own marriage in turmoil, they didn't know how to help themselves. When they asked to see Sherry and me, we prayed to see if the Lord wanted us to counsel them. After a week of praying, we felt that God had directed us to see them.

As we listened to the hurt and anger each felt toward the other, I knew it wasn't just the accumulation of fifteen years of marriage that had caused all the hurts. Each of them had come into the marriage with a load of pain from their own families. I explained that the process I use in marriage counselling is, first, to remove baggage from the past, then to solve the presenting issues they brought as a couple. Sherry and I met with Georgina first. We helped her untangle confusion and hurt from her past. At the same time, I met with Jim alone to hear his family background. As I often found, the perceptions he had of himself as a man were filled with distortions born of unresolved hurts from his father. His view of women was also distorted because he had witnessed how badly his father had treated his mother. That left him with a sense that women were not truly valued. Further, he was angry with his mother for her treatment of him as a boy, hanging onto him emotionally as he grew into manhood. He needed women, yet was afraid of them.

As we worked through the hurt and pain from the past, they both acknowledged the anger that had come from past hurts. As Jim and Georgina forgave their parents and others, we saw remarkable changes in their hearts. Jim took ownership of marital issues for which he had blamed Georgina. And Georgina, who seemed emotionally fragile and easily hurt, became willing to accept her part in the hurts of the marriage. Both of them saw the distorted view they held toward each other. They each began to understand and value their partner's marriage role. The learning curve they gained in solving their own marriage issues helped them significantly in working through other people's marriage problems.

Jim and Georgina's story is similar to other stories I have heard for years. The deep hurts within each person were hindering their perceptions of how to deal with their present marital issues. In fact, for many people, the hurts of life seldom get healed. As a result, hurts accumulate in their souls over a period of years. Gradually the 'emotional tank' gets full of pain. Then, after accumulating one too many hurts, they reach a crisis! The overload sends them crashing. They finally realize they need help to overcome their excessive emotional baggage.

All hurt, or emotional pain, represents danger. As we will see in the following pages, danger produces a natural reaction of anger. That is the way God has made us. To deal with the hurts of life, we must deal with stored anger in our emotions. To release buried anger, we must use the only key we have been given by God: forgiveness. So, in a nutshell, hurt produces anger and accumulated anger forms bitterness. Bitterness destroys our soul like cancer destroys the body. The only answer to this 'cancerous' bitterness is radical forgiveness. In this book, I want to take you on a journey of discovery: from hurt to anger to forgiveness and ultimately to freedom. May the Holy Spirit reveal the truth of his Word to each person reading these words.

So let's begin the process by exploring biblical truth about anger. Some of these truths about anger from the Scriptures may surprise you, because most of us carry misconceptions about anger and about the purpose for which anger is given to us.

Part 1

Anger's Purpose and Value

Chapter 1

Misconceptions of Anger

Because we have many and varied experiences of anger and hurts, we develop a false perception of what anger is. Most of our experiences have led us to believe that anger is bad, for this one simple reason: We confuse anger itself with the expression of anger. In the workshops that I have conducted over the years, I often ask my audience to define anger. A typical definition is this: Anger is an outburst of emotion, a fit of temper or someone expressing rage. Most people have great misconceptions of what anger really is. These misconceptions can be divided into four categories:

1. Anger is negative and destructive

Most of us don't like our experiences of anger expression, and therefore we think anger is bad. When, in our childhood, our parents mishandled their anger and yelled at us, hit us or punished us wrongly, we concluded that anger is bad. Isn't that our usual response to anger? Most of us have grown up with this kind of expression of anger in our families. During university graduate studies I was taught that anger is a neutral emotion. However, I learned through biblical study that anger is not primarily an emotion, although it certainly has emotional expression. In fact, anger is neither bad, nor neutral, but good. Because anger is often expressed in abuse, whether physical, emotional, verbal, sexual or spiritual, we think of anger as bad and therefore, negative and destructive. We need a major shift in our thinking about anger.

2. We are afraid of anger and think of it as our enemy

Because we perceive anger as negative, we fear and avoid it, in the same way we avoid angry people. This resulting view of anger commonly causes people to 'bury' it. In psychological terms, we say that anger is repressed or suppressed (repression is an unconscious process; suppression is a conscious process). Sometimes, when people are angry and are confronted by others about their anger, they deny being angry because it is generally not acceptable. Everyone has experienced this many times.

For example, we are at work. A colleague expresses a joking comment but it comes out as a derogatory statement. We laugh it off as we walk away but the statement hits like an arrow. In the busyness of our working day, we dismiss the comment (repress it) and get on with the day. Or, so we think. But our heart has been wounded and we carry this buried anger around throughout the day. Interestingly, the sarcasm we have just received from our colleague has probably come from his buried anger. So, we too pass the anger on to others again and again.

This process causes us to think of anger as an enemy. We do whatever we can to avoid it. We believe that anger is best kept under control. We try to manage our anger or skilfully protect ourselves from the anger of others. This idea of control is a myth, as you will see in our third misconception.

3. Anger should be totally controlled

Anger is often a difficult and confusing concept to understand. Because we don't understand it, we try to control it. We think that the best we can do with anger is to manage it. Managing anger expression is not wrong, but when we try to manage something we don't understand we often end up repressing it. It is like trying to put a fence around a vicious dog, thinking a fence will control it. When the dog gets frustrated enough, he will find a way to escape the fenced yard. When we attempt to control our anger, we are controlling the expression of anger without understanding why anger is there in the first place. Often, our attempt to manage anger is actually a way of burying it. It is correct that anger expression needs managing. And yes, anger expression can be managed properly, but that process will be discussed later.

We need to use anger for the purpose that God intended. That means learning how to manage the anger we express. But it also means much more. We must learn how to remove all the buried anger in us caused by the hurts of life, which have accumulated over years. In many relationships, we have unresolved issues that we carry around endlessly. Our failure to understand anger is the root of many destructive relationships, because we have learned to bury anger rather than to use it. Many of the hurtful comments we make to others come from our stored anger. Our usual control of anger is a vow not to say or do it again. Managing anger in this way is not effective in solving problems.

4. Our problems with anger are unique

Our fourth misconception about anger is that our struggles with anger are unique to us. Most of us are reluctant to talk about our feelings of anger. Imagine sitting at a social gathering and saying to someone you hardly know, 'So how have you handled your anger today?' Anger is a taboo subject, like death or sex. Anger is difficult to discuss, even with those close to you. Anger is a shame issue for us. We are ashamed to admit that we have angry feelings. When I have travelled to other countries to do workshops, I have found that the issue of anger is a problem in every culture. Handling anger is a concern for every family and individual around the world.

Anger expression is also generational. We learn to handle anger largely by the way our family handled anger. We express anger according to the way we have been raised. My father passed to me some of his wrong ways of expressing anger. He didn't do it intentionally. But the truth is, I learned how to express my anger by being the recipient of his anger. Of course, I passed my mistakes in handling anger on to my children. We all learn to use anger through past experiences. Yet we think that anger issues are unique to ourselves or to our family. But that is simply not true. The ways we express anger are common throughout the world.

Let's begin our discussion of anger by attempting to establish a biblical definition.

Chapter 2
Defining Anger

What is anger?

Despite the bad press anger has received, it is actually our friend, not our enemy. Anger is not bad or even neutral, but good. Anger is a gift from God (Judges 14:19). Anger enables us to defend ourselves against danger (Genesis 31:36). In fact, God himself gets angry when his children are hurt by others or diminished in any way. We refer to this as vicarious anger (Exodus 15:6–8). God's anger is expressed against sin, the devil and any enemy of ours. God is angry whenever his enemies try to hurt any of his children. God's expression of anger against our sin occurs because he knows how destructive sin is to his children. (Sin is defined as not living up to God's standard of holiness or perfection, which the Bible sets as the benchmark.) Sin is not only wrong, it also hurts us and destroys us. Because sin is destructive, it calls forth anger from God (1 Kings 11:9). If we are sinning against others, we often feel God's anger toward us for our destructive acts.

Parents certainly can understand God's perspective. Don't you as parents find anger rising if someone tries to harm your children? We may even experience greater anger when our children are attacked than when we ourselves are attacked. I remember when our oldest son Sam, who was about nine at the time, was playing in the playground behind our house. I walked out the back gate with my father-in-law, who was visiting, to see Sam. Walking past the trees that hid the play structure, I noticed an older boy sitting on the apparatus, spitting on Sam's head. Fortunately, my father-in-law was there to restrain me when immediate anger gripped me. I was ready to release unrestrained anger at this bully for the way he was treating my son.

The anger we feel when our children are under attack is from God, and is designed to protect us and our families from danger. Without anger to protect us, we would be hurt many times over and would have no means to defend ourselves. A person without the capacity to express or use anger to defend himself is victimized repeatedly.

Anger is from God

All human beings are made in the image of God (Genesis 1:27). We carry the likeness of God in our genes, albeit imperfectly because of the Fall. Within each of us is a built-in sense of justice and righteousness. We are keenly aware of someone violating our rights or treating us unfairly. The Creator himself has established these inherent rights in us. They express his design for our socialization and well-being. These rights include the right to justice, the right to dignity and honour, the right to meaningful purpose, and the right to act responsibly. When our rights have been violated, anger from God stirs an 'anger energy' in us to right the wrong. This authority to correct the wrong and defend the right is established by God in every human being.

In 2 Samuel 12, King David was confronted by the prophet Nathan about his sin against Uriah and Bathsheba. Nathan wisely told David a story about a rich man who took advantage of a poor man by slaughtering his one and only pet lamb for a supper for himself and his travelling guest. Verses 5–6 say, 'David burned with anger against the man and said to Nathan, "As surely as the Lord lives, the man who did this deserves to die! He must pay for that lamb four times over, because he did such a thing and had no pity."' Even though it was David who had sinned against God, the inherent sense of righteousness in David evoked his angry response when he heard this story from Nathan the prophet.

This same authority is given to parents to train, discipline and, when needed, punish their children. God defines the boundaries of right and wrong. God passes on his authority to parents, the church and the government to teach and maintain right and wrong. These boundaries, established by God's Word, help protect you and me from infringement on our rights. Proverbs 15:31–33 says, 'He who listens to a life-giving rebuke will be at home among the wise. He who ignores discipline despises himself, but whoever heeds correction gains understanding. The fear of the Lord teaches a man wisdom, and humility comes before honour.'

Anger is good

We know anger is good is because God himself expresses anger, yet he has no evil in him. He cannot be the sinless God of the Bible and have evil in himself. Because God is perfect in his holiness, the anger coming from God must be holy and right. We much prefer to think of God as 'love'. He is love, of course. However, God's anger in Scripture is expressed as much as his love. Anger and love are not mutually exclusive. We know we can be angry with the person we love the most. God expresses both anger and love toward his children, and both expressions are good.

We can see this in Psalm 90:11–14: 'Who knows the power of your anger? For your wrath is as great as the fear that is due you. Teach us to number our days aright, that we may gain a heart of wisdom. Relent, O Lord! How long will it be? Have compassion on your servants. Satisfy us in the morning with your unfailing love, that we may sing for joy and be glad all our days.' In Jeremiah 30:24 we also see the Lord using his anger to accomplish his loving purposes for his people, even when we don't understand it: 'The fierce anger of the Lord will not turn back until he fully accomplishes the purposes of his heart. In days to come you will understand this.' God always uses his anger to benefit his divine purposes.

God commands us to be angry

There is another reason why the Bible teaches that anger is good. Anger is good because God commands us to get angry, yet not sin in the expression of anger. Ephesians 4:26 tells us: 'Be angry and yet do not sin' (NASB). The Greek text is written in the present tense and the imperative mood. (The present tense in Greek means continuous action; the imperative mood is the voice of command.) This verse is a command to be obeyed continuously. Literally translated, it would read like this: 'I command you to be continuously angry [as needed] and yet continuously not to sin in your anger.' Why would God command us to be angry? Because he knows that we need anger to do what is right, and especially to stand against the enemy. Scripture never tells us to repress, suppress, deny or bury anger. Scripture demands that we use anger properly to accomplish God's purposes on the earth. We have been trained throughout our lives that anger is wrong. And we have been told to stop being angry, or even worse, to be ashamed of anger. Therefore, we automatically repress or bury many of our angry feelings. We simply do not understand God's purpose for anger.

God also commands us to forgive

The Bible also makes it clear that when our 'rights' have been violated and someone hurts us, we must also work through a process of forgiveness. Jesus said in Matthew 5:23–24: 'Therefore, if you are offering your gift at the altar and there remember that your brother has something against you, leave your gift there in front of the altar. First go and be reconciled to your brother; then come and offer your gift.' When we forgive our offender, we participate in Christ's redemptive process. We also verify that the offender's needs (from which the hurt derived) are important too. So, in forgiveness, we not only identify and accept our response to the hurt, but also we actively participate with Jesus in the redemptive healing of the person who caused the hurt. The Bible teaches a radical view of forgiveness. Matthew 6:14–15 says: 'For if you forgive men when they sin against you, your heavenly Father will also forgive you. But if you do not forgive men their sins, your Father will not forgive your sins.'

Forgiveness is not only for our well-being, but also for the healing of the nations. Only when we grasp the enormity of the debt from which we have been forgiven by God, can we become aware of how much and how often we wrong God and others. Christ's forgiveness is not just prescriptive, it is redemptive. He does not merely say, 'I forgive you', but he commits himself to our ongoing development. We are commanded to forgive in the same manner. We will have much more to say about forgiveness later in the book, but for now this helps establish the crucial nature of forgiveness in the Bible's discussion of anger and rights.

In order to further understand the Bible's view of anger, we need to get a clear definition of what anger actually is.

A definition of anger: A physiological response to danger

At its most basic level, anger can be defined as 'energy in our bodies designed to protect us from danger'. Here is how I arrived at this definition of anger. One day, when I was searching the Scriptures for answers for dealing with anger in relationships, I read this phrase a number of times: 'he burned with anger'. As I read the story in 1 Samuel 11:1–6, I saw something for the first time:

> *Nahash the Ammonite went up and besieged Jabesh Gilead. And all the men of Jabesh said to him, 'Make a treaty with us, and we will be subject to you.' But Nahash the Ammonite replied, 'I will make a treaty with you only on the condition that I gouge out the right eye of every one of you and so bring disgrace on all Israel.' The elders of Jabesh said to him, 'Give us seven days so we can send messengers throughout Israel; if no one comes to rescue us, we will surrender to you.' When the messengers came to Gibeah of Saul and reported these terms to the people, they all wept aloud. Just then Saul was returning from the fields, behind his oxen, and he asked, 'What is wrong with the people? Why are they weeping?' Then they repeated to him what the men of Jabesh had said. When Saul heard their words, the Spirit of God came upon him in power, and he burned with anger.*

Saul had just become the first king of Israel. He was not

well established as the ruling monarch yet. Israel's enemies harassed them at will. One enemy was the Ammonites, whose king was a bully. As Saul was walking from his fields one day, he met some people who were weeping loudly. He asked them what was wrong. Notice that when Saul heard the news, 'the Spirit of God came upon him in power, and he burned with anger'. God's power on Saul was expressed in his 'burning with anger'. God put his power into Saul. And Saul, motivated by this 'anger energy' from God, rallied the people to defeat this bullying king, winning the battle against the Ammonites.

Burning with anger

Notice the connection between 'the Spirit of God came upon him in power' and 'he burned with anger'. God energized Saul with power, using anger as the source of energy. Think about my definition of anger – energy in our bodies designed to protect us from danger. When you burn something, what happens? Energy is released in the form of heat and light. This phrase 'burned with anger' describes anger exactly. It is 'energy' in our bodies given by God to release power for protection from our enemies.

Interestingly, the words 'anger' and 'danger' are similar to each other in their etymology. (Only one letter differs between the two words.) The word 'danger' is defined as 'exposure to harm or evil'. The word 'anger' means 'the power to harm or protect'. Anger, of course, can be used either negatively or positively. But God intended us to use anger positively as 'energy' to protect us from danger. Anger is energy or power in our bodies that gives us strength for protection for ourselves or for others.

Walking down the back alley

Another illustration illuminates my definition. Suppose
that one night you decide to go to a local café for a
takeaway coffee. It's dark outside. You think to yourself,
'I should probably go by the well-lit route, but it's late
and I'm in a hurry to get back home.' So you walk down
a back alley to get to the café. On your way back through
the darkened alley, with your drink in your hand, you
sense something is not right. The apprehension you sense
is a form of fear: a warning signal that danger may be
lurking. (Fear is the emotional signal that warns us of the
possibility of danger.) You think you hear something, so
you strain to see if there is danger, but you see nothing.
Suddenly, someone jumps out from behind a fence with a
big knife and says, 'Give me your money' (or maybe your
coffee!).

At this point, the fear signal has pushed the 'anger
button', getting you ready for action. If fear has not
completely immobilized you, anger will energize your
body for action. At that point, a number of changes will
occur in you, automatically. Your heart rate will increase.
Your respiration rate will increase. Your skin temperature
will increase or decrease, depending on the need of the
moment. Your sweat glands will activate. Your muscles
will tense. Your digestive system will shut down. Your
mouth will go dry. Your pupils will enlarge. Blood will
flow to your extremities (hands and feet). Various glands
will activate to release hormones into your body.

These changes are autonomic (involuntary). In a
split second, without thinking about it, your body will
be ready for action. At that moment you will make an
instantaneous decision for 'flight or fight'. Do you use this
energy of anger to fight the attacker or do you run away

faster than you have ever run before? The energy of anger works to protect you from danger.

A medical perspective

I asked a good friend of mine, who is a medical doctor, to describe this anger reaction in the body from a medical viewpoint. Dr Mark Musk described it this way:

When we experience a strong emotional response like fear or rage, our body prepares for the 'flight or fight' response. Initially, the hypothalamus in the brain is activated through our perception of the environment; then, signals transmit through the reticular formation of the brainstem and into the spinal cord. The activation of the spinal cord causes massive sympathetic discharge at the nerve level, and hormone release. Hormones, like acetylcholine and norepinephrine, act primarily at the local level in tissues, while other hormones, including epinephrine, dopamine, corticosteroids, endorphins and glucagon act systemically. The result is increased blood flow to active muscles, an increase in blood glucose, free fatty acid concentrations and increased rates of cellular metabolism throughout the body. Our respiratory rate and heart rate increases and our pupils dilate to focus quicker. Our blood flow is shunted away from the gastrointestinal tract and kidneys. The reticular formation has a lower threshold for activation that leads to a reinforced alert or arousal rate, preparing the mind and body for action. In case of injury the blood clots more easily and blood vessels in the skin constrict during the response to limit bleeding from potential wounds. The truly amazing thing about the human body's response is the precision and the array of signals that prepares us for action.

When I read this technical, medical description of the body's response to stress, I thanked the Lord for how fearfully and wonderfully we are made!

A mother's anger energy

Some years ago, in a magazine on stress I read a true story about a woman who was watching her young son playing in the front yard of their house. He was playing with a little toy fire engine. The fire engine got away from him and went down the sloped driveway, heading for the street. The three-year-old chased his toy while the mother, watching from the window, gasped with concern. Just then, a van rounded the corner at high speed. The driver saw the little child heading out onto the street. He swerved to miss him and hit a telephone pole. The pole was knocked on top of the child's legs. Anger erupted in the mother at the van driver's carelessness. In the panic of the moment, she ran out to rescue her child. Without thinking, she lifted the telephone pole up to move it from her son's legs.

How did she have the strength to lift it? Was it fear or anger that energized her? It was the anger, aroused by danger to her child, that energized her to lift the heavy pole, saving her child's legs. We sometimes call this energy an 'adrenaline rush'. Without anger energy, she would not have been able to lift it. We probably wouldn't realize that this amazing strength came from her anger. But God intended anger to be used to protect us from danger. When danger occurs, the 'anger button' automatically signals us and we are energized to deal with the situation.

Danger to your self-esteem

Here is another illustration of anger. The previous illustrations refer to physical danger that arouses anger, but many other dangers are not physical in nature. Suppose you go to an office party. As you enjoy chatting with various colleagues, one of your office-mates sits beside you. You know he has a grudge against you, but this is a social occasion and you want to be friendly.

As the conversation continues, he becomes increasingly sarcastic and derogatory toward you. Because you are at a party, other people are part of the conversation. You keep your thoughts to yourself. You don't retaliate with sarcasm. But inside, you are aware that something is changing in your emotions. You are starting to 'burn'!

If we could test your body measurements at that moment, we would find your heart rate and respiration rate increased. Your muscles have tensed, you are perspiring and adrenaline is pumped into your system. In other words, your 'anger button' has been triggered. (It is probably not at the same level as in the back alley, but you are angry, nevertheless.) Even though you decline to express anger to this colleague because you want to avoid a scene, anger nevertheless has energized your body. In fact, you may be such a nice person that you are unaware that you are angry. But you are. Why? Because your office-mate's derogatory comments are dangerous to your self-esteem. His words are destructive to your emotional health and well-being. The inherent worth and value that God placed in you at your conception is being attacked.

The experience is similar to the back alley where you were threatened with a knife. But sarcasm is not as obvious a danger as the threat in the alley. Because you have been socialized not to retaliate in public, you will repress the anger, denying your angry feelings. However, when you leave that party you will feel something in your body – a tension that you did not have when you came. That tension is anger. The physiological response may be less dramatic, less noticeable, but anger has arisen in you for protection. God made you this way. Every time you experience danger or perceive danger, your body is energized through anger.

Anger and anger expression

Our confusion in understanding anger arises from our inability to distinguish between what anger is and how anger is expressed. This is a very important distinction! Most people think of anger in terms of its expression, which explains why anger is so often defined as rage. Anger, at its root, is 'energy' in our bodies, given by God to protect us from danger. Anger expression, however, becomes a more complex process. Anger expression is affected not only by the current issue that triggered it, but also by the accumulated anger in us over a period of years. It is very important to make a clear distinction between anger itself, and anger expression.

Let's look at 1 Samuel 20:28–34, a Scripture passage that distinguishes between anger and anger expression:

> *But the next day, the second day of the month, David's place was empty again. Then Saul said to his son Jonathan, 'Why hasn't the son of Jesse come to the meal, either yesterday or today?'*
>
> *Jonathan answered, 'David earnestly asked me for permission to go to Bethlehem. He said, "Let me go, because our family is observing a sacrifice in the town and my brother has ordered me to be there. If I have found favour in your eyes, let me get away to see my brothers."*

That is why he has not come to the king's table.'

Saul's anger flared up at Jonathan [burned against Jonathan – NASB] and he said to him, 'You son of a perverse and rebellious woman! Don't I know that you have sided with the son of Jesse to your own shame and to the shame of the mother who bore you? As long as the son of Jesse lives on this earth, neither you nor your kingdom will be established. Now send and bring him to me, for he must die!'

'Why should he be put to death? What has he done?' Jonathan asked his father. But Saul hurled his spear at him to kill him. Then Jonathan knew that his father intended to kill David. Jonathan got up from the table in fierce anger; on that second day of the month he did not eat, because he was grieved at his father's shameful treatment of David.

David and Saul

In the context of this story, David became a national hero in Israel because he had killed Goliath. Saul took David into his family and gave his daughter, Michal, to him for his wife. This previously unheard-of shepherd boy now ate his meals at the royal court. But as time went on, because of his insecurity, Saul felt threatened by David's popularity. (The more insecure we are, the more we perceive situations as dangerous to us.) Even David's close relationship with Jonathan became a threat to Saul. Both David and Jonathan were aware of the danger to David. Since Saul had already attempted to kill David with his spear on two different occasions, David thought that eating with the king was dangerous to his health. David and Jonathan developed an excuse for David to miss this meal. David planned to visit his father in Bethlehem for a family celebration. But Saul saw through this ruse and his anger flared up at Jonathan.

Saul exploded in rage toward Jonathan, his son, because he felt threatened by David. He felt that Jonathan was himself being duped by David in giving up his right of succession to the throne. Saul's anger was so out of control that he even tried to kill his own son with a spear. Notice Jonathan's response. He too became angry because his father's anger was a danger to him and to his friendship with David. But Jonathan refused to use his anger to dishonour his father by retaliating against him. Instead he used his anger to remove himself from the danger at the dinner table. He carried out his plan to save his friend, David. The injustice of Saul's treatment of David caused anger to rise in Jonathan. This anger energized Jonathan to risk his life to save David's. That is using anger appropriately. Anger can be expressed either destructively or constructively. It is our choice. But anger itself is good when it is used as God intended – to protect us or others from danger.

Chapter 3

How Anger Expresses Itself Outwardly

Now let's examine the common ways for expressing our anger. These expressions of anger are usually the result of the anger we have buried (or repressed) through a period of years. Two of these expressions of anger are directed outward, toward others, and two of them are directed inward, toward ourselves. The expression we most often associate with anger is rage.

People who express anger outwardly toward other people view these people as dangerous to themselves. Most likely, they have had this expression of anger modelled to them by significant people in their lives. No one told them that rage is how you should express anger. They learned about rage because they lived with it and became victims of rage as they were growing up.

Rage (active anger)

Most of us think that anger is rage and rage is anger. When we describe an angry person, we usually mean they have a problem with uncontrolled rage. This is also referred to as active anger or active aggression. When we see acts of physical abuse, verbal abuse or sexual abuse, we recognize these acts as anger. When a person swears at others, yells or threatens violence, we are witnessing expressions of rage. Acts of vandalism, insults and rudeness are all expressions of rage or active aggression. We refer to these acts of violence as anger, yet they are really *expressions* of anger rather than anger itself.

One of the increasing expressions of rage in our society is road rage. Pent-up anger can sometimes reach a boiling-point while people are driving. The car then becomes a lethal weapon able to destroy lives. Sometimes people get out of their vehicles so full of rage that they explode in a flurry of fists at another driver. I remember an incident in Calgary, Alberta, when I was driving through the city on Crowchild Trail. One driver had cut off another in traffic. When they reached the next set of traffic lights, they got out of their vehicles and started fighting.

If you want to determine whether you are an angry driver, take the survey in Appendix 1 at the end of the book.

A biblical example of rage

In 2 Chronicles 16:7–10 we find a biblical example of rage, when the prophet Hanani gave King Asa a rebuke from the Lord he did not want to hear:

> At that time Hanani the seer came to Asa king of Judah and said to him: 'Because you relied on the king of Aram and not on the Lord your God, the army of the king of Aram has escaped from your hand. Were not the Cushites and Libyans a mighty army with great numbers of chariots and horsemen? Yet when you relied on the Lord, he delivered them into your hand. For the eyes of the Lord range throughout the earth to strengthen those whose hearts are fully committed to him. You have done a foolish thing, and from now on you will be at war.'
>
> Asa was angry with the seer because of this; he

was so enraged that he put him in prison. At the same time Asa brutally oppressed some of the people.

Asa, generally a good king, lost control of himself in his rage, becoming a tyrant. Probably all of us have experienced an Asa-type outburst sometime in our life and have lived to regret it.

Most of us incorrectly call anger rage, but it is not. Rage is only one of four expressions of anger. Passive aggression (or passive anger) is the next expression of anger we will examine.

Passive aggression (passive anger)

Because rage is commonly thought of as anger, many are unfamiliar with passive expressions of anger. Amazingly, passive aggression is actually the most common expression of anger directed toward others. Perhaps, due to the numerous ways in which we express anger passively, we seem to get away with it. Moreover, passive expressions of anger are socially more acceptable than rage. Most people feel safer expressing their anger subversively rather than directly. Here are some examples of passive anger:

Gossip

Gossip is a form of anger. You may ask, 'How is that?' Suppose you are angry at a friend, but you are afraid to confront him directly with your anger. Instead of telling your friend to his face that you are angry, you tell someone else what you think of your friend. When you do this, you are using an indirect approach to express your anger. By discussing someone else's negative qualities you have retaliated for the anger you feel. What you are doing is assassinating the character of your friend by gossiping about him to someone else. That is a passive (and subtle) form of anger. 'He who conceals his hatred has lying lips, and whoever spreads slander is a fool' (Proverbs 10:18).

This verse says that when we slander or gossip about someone out of an intense dislike of him, we have not properly resolved our anger toward him. As a result, we are living a lie. The reason we slander or gossip is because we have buried anger toward that person. The Bible teaches that when we use gossip or slander we function as a fool. A fool lives as if God is not an active part of his life. Psalm 14:1 says: 'The fool says in his heart, "There is no God."' In essence we are saying we won't have to give an account for slandering someone because that person may not hear it. But God surely has heard, and he will hold us accountable for expressing our anger wrongfully.

Procrastination

Procrastination (postponing or delaying needlessly) is another way of expressing passive anger. Some (but, obviously, not all) procrastination is rooted in buried anger. Here's an example:

In one of my employment situations, I once supervised several employees. This came about because a new position was created in the department. I applied for the position and was the first person to take on this role. Being a novice, I had lots to learn in this new job. When I first wrote the employees' annual evaluations, I focused on the negative side of their performance rather than the positive. As a result, one of the employees was upset with me. Soon afterwards, she began arriving at work just on time but eventually a few minutes late. This was not her typical behaviour. She was normally a person who arrived fifteen to twenty minutes early. She knew that procrastinating behaviour bothered me because I liked the employees to be ready for people when the doors to the centre opened.

So, I finally asked this employee to come to my office. I told her I sensed her anger, asking her what was wrong. She told me that she thought I was unfair in my evaluation and felt I did not appreciate her. So we discussed her evaluation again and I apologized. She returned to her old pattern of coming to work early and was an excellent employee during my years as chairman of the department.

You often see procrastination as an anger expression in children. If you're a parent, you probably know the scenario. When you call your children for supper, they don't respond. They are engrossed in their play and are not interested in being disturbed. You call them for supper a second time, a third time, and finally, as the decibels in your voice rise, the children respond to the invitation to join you for supper. Their procrastination comes from the anger they feel at being disturbed during playtime: 'How dare Mum (or Dad) disturb me when I'm having such a good time?'

It is not the anger in the child that is bad. Anger is the child's natural response to perceived danger ('Mummy, you're disturbing my playtime'). Whether the child responds with either rebellion against or submission to his/her parents, becomes the defining issue. Teaching and disciplining the child at this stage in his/her life sets the foundation for future issues of procrastination in school, work and relationships. Of course, husbands and wives can use the same passive expression of anger when they don't want to go shopping or camping or whatever. We often overlook this anger because it is not rage but a low-level anger expressed in a passive manner.

Having said this, we also need to recognize that some

procrastination may arise from bad habits formed over time. It may have started as passive anger but now is a habit pattern that has become part of our lifestyle. Often these habits can only be broken through the conscious effort of restructuring our thinking and resetting our internal clocks. Getting to church or work on time may require a conscious process of rethinking every step we take to leave home. If procrastination is rooted in anger from long ago, go back in your memory, asking the Holy Spirit to show you where the anger started years ago. But please, please, whatever you do, don't diagnose everyone you meet who is late for events as having a buried anger issue! Work on your own issues rather than those of others.

Sarcasm

Another common passive expression of anger is sarcasm. People often use sarcasm to express anger toward others or toward life in general. The English word 'sarcasm' comes from the Greek word *sarkazein*, which means 'to tear the flesh'. Sarcasm communicates contempt or mocking, designed to leave a person unsure of your meaning. Is it a compliment or not? Sometimes the contempt intended is clear, like tearing the flesh off someone, but often sarcasm leaves the person confused as to the intended meaning. For example, 'I just love your new hairdo' can be said with sincerity or 'dripping' with sarcasm. You will usually find that when you are angry toward your spouse or another person, sarcasm comes out frequently and blatantly. When you find yourself using sarcasm, allow the Holy Spirit to show you what lies behind it.

A biblical example of sarcasm can be seen in Nehemiah 4:1–5. In this context, the Jews are busy rebuilding the walls of Jerusalem, to the chagrin of their enemies – particularly two men named Sanballat and Tobiah:

> *When Sanballat heard that we were rebuilding the wall, he became angry and was greatly incensed. He ridiculed the Jews, and in the presence of his associates and the army of Samaria, he said, 'What are those feeble Jews doing? Will they restore their wall? Will they offer sacrifices? Will they finish in a day? Can they bring the stones back to life from those heaps of rubble – burned as they are?'*
>
> *Tobiah the Ammonite, who was at his side, said, 'What they are building – if even a fox climbed up on it, he would break down their wall of stones!'*
>
> *Hear us, O our God, for we are despised. Turn their insults back on their own heads. Give them over as plunder in a land of captivity. Do not cover up their guilt or blot out their sins from your sight, for they have thrown insults in the face of the builders.*

Can't you hear the dripping sarcasm in their voices as they express anger toward the Jews for daring to rebuild the walls of Jerusalem? Of course, not all sarcasm is necessarily rooted in anger. Sometimes it can simply be good jesting between friends. However, if you use sarcasm a great deal, you should look for roots of buried anger from the past.

Teasing

A fourth example of passive anger is teasing. It is obvious that some teasing is just good-natured fun. As long as everybody enjoys it, teasing can be an expression of trust and friendship within a group or family. However, teasing can also come from buried anger. Most of us have had experiences of unmerciful teasing, to the point of crying or deeply hurting.

As I am writing this I realize I need to make a confession. I am a terrible tease! Because my maternal grandfather was also a great tease, I often justify my teasing as inherited. However, I am also aware of growing up with buried anger (which I wasn't aware of at the time). In retrospect, I realize I aimed my anger at my younger twin sisters, Lynne and Elaine. As a twin myself, I struggled with feelings of inferiority toward my brother, Grant (no fault of his). One way of dealing with my feelings of inferiority was to cause trouble for someone else in the family. (I was not conscious of this process.) This may sound perverse, but I would feel better when I teased my sisters to the point of aggravation. This teasing arose from roots of bitterness, even though I wasn't particularly on bad terms with my two younger sisters.

I also noticed this phenomenon with my own children. My three older children learned to express anger in a passive way through teasing; the two younger ones picked up the same trait. Now, I know what you are thinking: this is a generational response to my being such a tease (and you may be right). I suspect it is also human nature. When one of our younger sons gets a lecture from Dad or Mum, he will sometimes tease his brother in the hope of causing him trouble. When children get themselves into trouble, they love to share the misery of it with their siblings. Aren't children thoughtful in their sharing! Misery does love company.

Pouting

Pouting is another expression of passive anger. Pouting is used to spoil someone's day when we are angry with him or her. We use pouting as a pay-back when we are angry over not getting our way. Children often display pouting.

When they don't get their way with parents, siblings or friends, they withdraw emotionally by pouting. The pouting child's bottom lip sticks out and there is a pseudo-hurt look on his or her face. But guess what? Many adults are pouters, too.

Once I was counselling a couple in my office. We were working through a backlog of buried anger between them. In the midst of the counselling they told me that the next weekend they were going to visit the wife's family in Great Falls, Montana. I could tell from the husband's non-verbals that he disliked visiting his in-laws. The wife had really wanted this trip and had badgered her husband to take the time off work. So, he finally agreed to go. Apparently, he pouted the whole weekend. He made the weekend miserable for his wife. When they came back for their next counselling session, the wife was really angry over her husband's behaviour. The husband rather smugly pointed out his wife's problem with anger. Unfortunately he failed to see his own anger, expressed in the form of pouting.

Non-compliance

One of the most common expressions of passive anger is non-compliance. It can be observed in situations where people are asked to do something they don't want to do. Anger arises because what they are required to do does not fit their interest or desire. So they express this anger in a passive way by simply not complying. For example, the boss at work asks you to write a letter or make a phone call on his behalf. You don't do it because of your anger at being asked to do something that you don't like. We can see this in children, as well. Often non-compliance with parents' requests is a form of anger at being asked to do something they don't like to do. They stall and stall on obeying the request from father or mother. Only after repeated calls from the parent does the child obey. Other examples of non-compliance might include a husband not responding to his wife's request to fix a household item, or a wife's unwillingness to cook the husband's favourite meal. The simmering anger in each of them feeds their unwillingness to cooperate with each other.

Bad driving habits

We also see passive anger expressed in our driving habits. Many people can relate to this scenario. You are driving down the street in your city when someone pulls out in front of you. However, they are not going close to the speed limit and you are in a hurry to get to a meeting. You 'sit' on their bumper and say things under your breath (or maybe not under your breath!). You cannot pass them and they seem oblivious to the fact that they are slowing you down. You sense your temperature rising and are aware of the tension in your whole body. Finally, after blocks of following this car, you get a chance to pass. Then you slow down, forcing him to go even slower. Now I know that neither you nor I would ever do that. But even if we haven't done it, we would like to, at times – right? The aggressive response would be to run that person off the road. Fortunately, most of us have a better grip on our anger. But the passive approach has difficulties, including a bad effect on our blood pressure.

Enuresis

Passive anger can be seen in children who wet or soil their pants. Not all issues of bedwetting (enuresis) are anger-based, but some are. It is worth checking to see if the issue is rooted in buried anger.

Joy was a single mother. Her alcoholic husband had left her and she was overwhelmed with raising three children. The father moved to another city and rarely visited the children or showed interest in them. Joy was feeling rejected, deserted, hurt and angry. The children were feeling the same, but the middle child, Johnny, seemed most affected by the father's absence. Joy often expressed her anger to the children and 'number two' again seemed to be the hardest hit. The mother got involved with another man. She had a child by this man; thus Johnny, now six years old, had to cope with another member in the family. At this same time, Johnny began having problems with night-time bedwetting, eventually escalating into daytime wetting and soiling his underwear. Imagine Joy's anger at the shame of going to the school again and again to bring fresh clothes because her son smelled bad with his soiled pants. The whole class complained about her Johnny.

This was getting to be a very difficult problem and the social workers seemed to have no solutions. One of the questions that needed to be answered was whether this was a physical or an emotional problem. They determined that it was not primarily a physical issue. With Joy's permission, Johnny was taken from the home for the summer. When he was placed with a Christian family for six weeks, he only soiled once and wet once. Then Johnny was placed in another home for three weeks, and in that time he never soiled at all and only wet himself once. By the time the summer was over, it was clear that Johnny was very angry with his father and his mother. He wrongly blamed his mother for the loss of his father and the loss of his place in the family. When Joy and Johnny received counselling, they were able to re-unite in the home, with the soiling and wetting virtually stopped.

Johnny was angry but had no way to express his anger

directly, without a verbal lashing from his mother. He had no way of expressing anger toward his father who had deserted him. He stored a lot of anger. Eventually, he expressed his anger through enuresis and soiling himself. As Johnny was able to work out the anger toward his mother and father, his need to express anger in a passive state disappeared.

Poor school performance

I have seen anger expressed passively in children who were not doing well in school. Because poor performance in school can be related to numerous issues, it is important to check other possibilities first. Having examined issues like IQ level, peer pressure, teacher conflict, test anxiety or a generalized fear in a group setting, then consider the possibility of a passive-anger issue. Is the child expressing his anger toward his parents or the teacher by poor school work?

Once I was counselling a fourteen-year-old boy whom a social worker had brought in. After a few sessions I gained his trust. Eventually, he told me his story. However, I sensed he was not telling the whole story because some things seemed amiss. Eventually, he confided a very painful experience he had had as a younger child.

He said, 'When I was seven years of age, living at home with my parents and my older brother and sister, my father took the family to the garage with a loaded rifle pointed at us all.' He stood the family up against one of the walls and paced back and forth saying, 'Should I kill you or should I not?'

This went on for several hours and finally he put the gun away and released the family. This incident was never talked about in the family and never reported to anyone.

Eventually the mother divorced the father and remarried.

This young man had carried a deep fear and anger for seven years, with no emotional outlet. No wonder he had anger issues toward authority expressed in the home and the school. With his permission, I told his mother and step-father. We began working out his deep-seated anger toward his biological father. After he had released his anger, his passive behaviour of doing poorly in school stopped and he went on to perform well.

Shoplifting

Shoplifting also expresses passive anger. It is an indirect way of expressing anger toward the 'system' or toward authority either in the home or in society. By stealing, the person is saying: 'I am angry at not having what I want. I have the right to take whatever I want that pleases me.' Sometimes shoplifting indirectly pays back an authority figure in the family through embarrassment, using shame as a weapon.

Here is an example. A father brought his fifteen-year-old son for counselling. The father was a high-ranking member of the police. When the son was caught shoplifting, the father, because of his anger, only made conditions worse. The son was slow to trust the counsellor, since he had not come for counselling voluntarily. He viewed the counsellor as another authority figure, like his father. Because he was so angry with his father, he didn't divulge his thoughts and emotions to anyone else. However, the counsellor eventually won his trust. The son began to describe how belittled his father made him feel. His authoritarian father ran the home with the same expectations that he had for the police officers under his command. At home, none of the family was allowed to express dissent or give feedback. So this son was full of anger for the way his father treated him, his brother and his sister.

The son only felt safe to express anger passively. One day, he went with friends to the shopping centre, where he got caught shoplifting. This was not a conscious, well-thought-out plan by this young man. Although being caught was unintentional, he didn't seem to mind when he was caught. When the police officer brought him home, his father was angry and embarrassed about his son's behaviour. When the counsellor pointed out that he was paying back his father by this behaviour, the boy had no trouble acknowledging that this was right. As they worked out his anger toward his father, the boy was able to forgive him and change his angry attitude. When the counsellor suggested to the father that he needed counselling as well, he responded with the statement, 'I'm paying you to get my son better, not me!'

Excessive spending of money

I noted another example of passive-aggressive behaviour while counselling a wife whose husband had left her. At issue was excessive spending by the woman's son. Initially, I was counselling the wife but I saw the husband on a couple of occasions. Then the husband left his wife of twenty-six years for another woman. She was devastated. She was deeply hurt and angry at his betrayal. There was one child remaining at home, a seventeen-year-old son who was to start his last year at school in the autumn. He worked all summer to save money, principally because he wanted to buy a car. The mother, unknowingly, controlled her son out of hurt and anger toward her husband. The son was becoming increasingly angry with his mother but would not express it to her because he could see the depth of her hurt from his father.

When the summer ended, in one weekend the son spent the entire $2,000 he had saved on an expensive holiday. His mother was furious. When she came to the next session, she asked what was wrong with her son. Why would he do such a thing? I gently suggested that the cause might have to do with her son's anger toward her for her excessive control over him. She reacted with anger toward me. As we examined this issue, I assured her that her anger toward her ex-husband was right and justified because of his betrayal. But how she expressed her anger was wrong. Her son paid the price for her misdirected anger. Fortunately, she saw the issues and continued working through her significant anger toward her ex-husband. Eventually, she lowered her controls on her son's life. Working out anger in a therapeutic manner enabled her to reduce her need to be in complete control, and she saved her relationship with her son.

Adultery

Another common expression of passive anger is marital infidelity. One spouse, angry with the other spouse, doesn't deal with his or her anger directly. Instead, the offended spouse uses adultery to pay back the other spouse for the anger he or she feels. This expression of passive anger is common in our culture today.

A travelling evangelist visited a church to hold meetings. Because of the strong presence of the Lord, the church asked him to stay a few more weeks. A kind and warm-hearted man, he gave his time to listen to people. A woman in the church (the wife of one of the pastors) was especially drawn to this evangelist because of his warm, caring heart. Before she knew it, she was having an affair with him. Because her husband was so busy in his ministry in the church, he neglected his wife emotionally. He loved his work and, in essence, was married to the church. The wife's growing resentment toward her husband and the church opened the door for the evangelist to exploit her need for affection. She took out her anger toward her husband by committing adultery. Naturally, such a major crisis in the church required a couple of years to resolve their marriage and the pastor's ministry.

Bill and Janet were married for fifteen years. For the first ten years, the marriage seemed cordial. Bill appreciated Janet's love of life but he hated her need to be in control. Then Bill had an affair. He had been storing anger in himself for years because he didn't know how to express it to her in direct terms. He saw her as dominant and controlling but did not know how to deal with it. Two years later, Janet had an affair. She paid Bill back for his adultery. Their counsellor at the time heard the story of the two affairs. He said to them, 'You're both even now, so forget it and get on with life.' Five years later they received counselling again, because of constant anger with each other. They paid each other back but deep anger remained.

The untangling process involved not only their current marriage issues, but also past issues that each of them brought into the marriage from their families of origin. Bill's general view of women was influenced by his childhood family. His father, a successful businessman, was 'addicted to acceptance' and needed recognition wherever he went. As a result of his father's neglect, Bill formed an emotional bond with his mother, who dominated him and over-protected him. When Bill looked for a mate, he chose someone like his mother, a dominant woman who would take care of him, providing for all his needs. Of course, Bill didn't recognize this internalized response at the time – he just felt comfortable with the familiar. However, as time passed, Bill became increasingly angry at Janet's control and bossiness.

Janet came from a family with a domineering father who had little respect for his wife or women in general. Janet vowed never to marry a man like her father. She looked for a man who was gentle, passive and affectionate. Bill was everything she was looking for in a man (including the fact that he was very handsome). Eventually she tired of this passive man who never took the initiative in the relationship. He would consistently withdraw into his work and the world of sports. Dealing with the hurts of their past families, as well as their marital hurts, meant a long process of working through necessary forgiveness.

Mocking

I have also observed mocking as another form of passive anger. In one marriage counselling session, the passive anger expressed by the wife to her husband was seen in constant mocking, causing him to look stupid. The wife, a Christian, attended an evangelical church regularly. The husband was not a Christian. He stated quite clearly that he didn't need God, especially if God was anything like his wife. She appeared self-righteous. When she criticized him, he expressed his anger inappropriately by yelling at her and then withdrawing emotionally for days. His yelling convinced her she was justified in her unwillingness to submit to her husband. After all, he wasn't a Christian and he was full of anger. Pulling the rug out from under him, again and again, she wondered why he showed no interest in her and her faith. Unfortunately, she was unable to see her own passive anger in the relationship. She drove him away from her until he divorced her.

A biblical example

A classic biblical example of passive anger is found in 1 Kings 21:1–7:

> *Some time later there was an incident involving a vineyard belonging to Naboth the Jezreelite. The vineyard was in Jezreel, close to the palace of Ahab king of Samaria. Ahab said to Naboth, 'Let me have your vineyard to use for a vegetable garden, since it is close to my palace. In exchange I will give you a better vineyard or, if you prefer, I will pay you whatever it is worth.'*
>
> *But Naboth replied, 'The Lord forbid that I should give you the inheritance of my fathers.'*
>
> *So Ahab went home, sullen and angry because Naboth the Jezreelite had said, 'I will not give you the inheritance of my fathers.' He lay on his bed sulking and refused to eat.*
>
> *His wife Jezebel came in and asked him, 'Why are you so sullen? Why won't you eat?'*
>
> *He answered her, 'Because I said to Naboth the Jezreelite, "Sell me your vineyard; or if you prefer, I will give you another vineyard in its place." But he said, "I will not give you my vineyard."'*
>
> *Jezebel his wife said, 'Is this how you act as king over Israel? Get up and eat! Cheer up. I'll get you the vineyard of Naboth the Jezreelite.'*

King Ahab was a pathetic excuse for a man. When he couldn't get his way with righteous Naboth, he sulked, refusing to eat. This is a classic case of passive anger. Queen Jezebel, his anything-but-passive wife, heard that Ahab was sulking and not eating. She was outraged. 'You're the king – don't you know? You can have whatever you want. If you can't figure out how to get his vineyard, I'll do it for you.' She took charge, setting up a 'kangaroo court' for Naboth, then had him executed. Ahab has gone down in history as a passive, wimpy man. Passive anger has fooled many people through the ages. They fail to see their passiveness as anger expression. Therefore they never deal with the root of it.

Chapter 4

How Anger Expresses Itself Inwardly

Both active aggression (rage) and passive aggression are outward anger expressions toward others. But these are not the only ways to express anger. Sometimes insecurity and fear of rejection are so strong that people can't or won't express their anger outwardly to others. Instead, they turn anger on themselves. This anger can be expressed in the mind (against one's self-esteem) or in the body (through psychosomatic illnesses). Let's examine these two expressions of anger.

Anger expressed in the mind (against one's self-esteem)

We can express our inward anger against ourselves, by telling ourselves that we are no good. By concentrating on what is wrong with ourselves, rather than what is right, criticizing ourselves and putting ourselves down, we are expressing anger inwardly.

I remember an incident in high school that illustrates this type of anger. I was rather insecure and shy during my school years. Even in the higher grades, I seldom volunteered answers in the class. Once, one of my teachers asked the class for answers to some reading homework she had assigned. Scouring the room, she chose me. I froze, because I had not done my homework. I gave her an answer I thought was right. In fact, I was rather proud of my answer, as I recall. However, my response was so wrong that the students burst into gales of laughter and I was left thoroughly red-faced. I never intended it to be a joke and would have loved the attention if I had meant it as a joke, because I loved making people laugh. But at that moment I felt so stupid, ashamed and awkward for having shared my ridiculous answer. I remember saying, quietly to myself, 'What an idiot I am! I should have kept my big mouth shut and pleaded insanity (or something).' Have you ever done that? I know we all have, probably many times in our growing years (maybe we still do it). We are attacking ourselves with our anger.

I realized I was very angry with my teacher for requiring me to answer the question. But if I had taken my anger out on the teacher, I would have been in even worse trouble than I was in for failing to do my homework. If I had taken my anger out on my classmates, they would have turned on me in a worse way than laughing at me. So where was the only safe place to express my anger? Obviously, I had to express it toward myself.

I don't like me

Many people respond similarly when making a mistake or when experiencing a personal failure despite fervent attempts to succeed. What are they doing? They are directing anger at themselves. They call themselves names, like 'imbecile', 'half-wit', 'dummy' and worse (but we don't want to put those in print, do we?!). If someone else called them such names, they would be insulted and angry. Yet they call themselves names but don't realize what they are doing.

If they repeat this name-calling over time, they will

believe their own internal messages, thus causing their self-esteem to lower. What they are telling themselves in this internalized anger is that they don't like themselves, especially when making mistakes or experiencing failure. They are angry with others, but are directing it to themselves. The lower their self-esteem, the more likely they are to withdraw from others whom they think will dislike them. After all, if they don't like themselves, why would anyone else like them? They project an image which says, 'If you really knew me you wouldn't like me, because I don't like myself.'

The negative tape recorder

In my *Healing Life's Hurts* workshops I often describe inward anger as listening to a negative 'tape recorder' being played over and over in the mind. When you push the 'On' button, it plays a message saying how dumb, stupid, inadequate and foolish you are. Then, when you next make a mistake or experience difficulty, the 'tape recorder' turns on again. You are not doing any of this consciously. This unconscious process happens whether you are aware of it or not. Just think about it. It is as if you are brainwashing yourself. If another person repeatedly tells you that you are stupid, you will eventually believe it. The same is true when you tell yourself the same message.

Turning anger inward develops a sense of inadequacy or helplessness in us. We may feel unable to take on new challenges; we can barely meet our daily needs. When this internal message of inadequacy becomes so ingrained, we begin living our self-imposed message. This internalized anger can even lead us to deliberately fail. We don't fail consciously, of course, but failure happens nonetheless.

Mr and Mrs Jones struggled with anger from their oldest daughter, Susan. She had just entered college after receiving promising academic marks in high school. During her first semester, great anger surfaced in this young lady, directed at her parents. By the second semester, she was doing poorly in her studies, after doing exceptionally well in her first semester. Her parents questioned the poor performance. They received a third-party perspective through seeing a family counsellor. They discovered a significant amount of anger in Susan that had never surfaced in her earlier years. The parents had seen their daughter's potential and promise. But, without realizing it, they had pushed her constantly to achieve well. Susan, who loved her parents and didn't want to take her anger out on them, took it out on herself. By expressing her anger inwardly, she viewed herself as a failure and, as a result, functioned destructively at college.

Accident proneness

Surprisingly, internalized anger is expressed in another way – accident proneness. The message gets expressed in this way: 'I am worthless – so why should I care for myself?' This attitude is not conscious masochism but unconscious carelessness, which can lead to numerous accidents.

I met a woman (we'll call her Mary) who was working as a colleague. She came to work late once, which was not typical behaviour. I said, 'I see you are late this morning, Mary. Did something happen to you?'

She replied, somewhat off-handedly, 'Oh, I had another accident.'

I picked up on the word 'another' because of the way she said it. I asked her, '*Another* accident?'

She replied, 'It's my eighth accident in three years.'

I immediately realized this accident was more than just 'another one'. I asked Mary if she wanted to discuss it sometime when it was more convenient. She replied that she would. Later, as we talked, I enquired about her multiple accidents over the three years. I asked Mary why she thought she was having so many car accidents. She really didn't understand why she had such bad luck.

Mary – a bright, intelligent woman and a very gifted, well-coordinated athlete – was not a 'klutz'. I asked if she would tell me her story. She was the second of two children, having an older sister. Her father, also an exceptional athlete, received numerous honours for his athletics. When Mary was born, her father expressed openly that he had wanted a boy to follow in his footsteps. He wanted his daughter to be the son that he never had. So in order to please her father, Mary tried to become the son he wanted. As a result, she followed in his athletic ways. Although he was a kind man and a good father, there remained an undercurrent of his desire for a son. When Mary was in her early twenties, her father died, leaving this issue unresolved. But the hurt remained buried in Mary's psyche.

As I listened, I realized that, despite her many qualifications and natural abilities, Mary saw herself as inadequate. Subconsciously, she remained angry at both herself and her father for this impossible situation. She strived to be the perfect son, yet she wasn't a son at all. She could never become the son he wished for. Her accident-proneness resulted from internalized anger.

I said, 'I believe you are angry at your father.'

She quickly disputed this assessment: 'Oh, no – you don't understand. I love my father more than anyone else!'

I told her, 'I know you love him, but I believe you are

very angry at him.' As I explained the impossible dilemma her father had imposed on her by wanting her to be a boy, she saw where her anger originated. Her father never accepted her as his daughter. He always wanted her to be someone she could not be. As Mary worked out her anger, her perspective on herself and her identity changed.

Depression – the big one

In my estimation, the most common and most devastating expression of anger turned inward is depression. Many psychologists believe depression is epidemic in society. Both chronic depression (often referred to as unipolar depression) and bipolar depression (formerly called manic depression) are serious behavioural disorders. Bipolar depression is characterized by periods of deep lows and extreme highs. The depressed person, after a while, attempts to withdraw from the depression by manic behaviour. Manic behaviour begins with excessive energy, but when it dissipates, the person slides into another deep depression.

Depression is a complex emotional/behavioural disorder. Over time, the emotional ups and downs create a change in the chemistry of the brain. These chemical changes are the major cause for unipolar and bipolar depression. That is why the medical community's treatment of choice for unipolar and bipolar illnesses is various antidepressants. However, I keep asking myself what causes the chemistry of the brain to change. I don't want to be simplistic in describing it, but I want to communicate clearly what a depression feels like.

Depression is like a hole in the ground – like an old well, not completely dry at the bottom. Depression feels like someone lowering you into that old, abandoned well with a rope, then removing the rope. The bottom of the well is wet and muddy and you feel like you're stuck up to your knees in gooey slime. In the Bible, the prophet Jeremiah literally had this experience: 'So they took Jeremiah and put him into the cistern of Malkijah, the king's son, which was in the courtyard of the guard. They lowered Jeremiah by ropes into the cistern; it had no water in it, only mud, and Jeremiah sank down into the mud' (Jeremiah 38:6).

Stretching out, you feel the walls around you. They feel like they are closing in on you. You look up to see a light in the distance but it is a 'lo-o-o-ong' way up. You feel there is no hope of getting out, unless someone rescues you. However, you believe no one cares enough or knows what you are going through. A sense of hopelessness begins to pervade your thinking. You experience anger, fear and shame. In a state of depression, this is how people feel.

How does a person fall into a depression in the first place? Think about it this way. If you continue criticizing yourself (being angry at yourself), 'putting yourself down' over a long period of time, what are you doing? You dig yourself into a hole, deeper and deeper. If you criticize yourself persistently, the hole gets so deep that you will have difficulty getting out. Through years of working with depressed clients, I have found a root of buried anger in each person. When they accumulate life's hurts, which have never healed, the resulting anger stores in the psyche. Eventually, they enter a state of depression, full of internalized anger.

Val's story

Once I counselled a woman in her early forties. Val had been in a depression for twenty years. She had attempted suicide at least four times and was taking antidepressants. Val had consulted a number of psychiatrists who treated her depression with drugs. Divorced and living in the same city as her mother, Val's initial concern was an ongoing conflict with her mother. I counselled her weekly over two years. Deeply hurt, angry and depressed, Val sometimes cried through half of the counselling session. Often I felt her pain and hopelessness so deeply that I wept with her. Frequently, I felt unable to help Val. I prayed many times, 'God, please help me find answers for Val.' In listening to her pain, I was looking for direction to help overcome her long and deep depression.

As she shared her painful story, I sensed that a root of buried anger from her past was key in this untangling process. However, often my search was interrupted by another 'pressing' problem in her present circumstances. These interruptions added confusion to her depression. Years earlier, Val experienced rejection when her husband divorced her. Since then, most of the relationships she experienced with men failed. Ultimately, she suffered rejection many times. She never kept a relationship with a man for long. On top of being angry with her mother, she was also angry at God. From her perspective, God had deserted her repeatedly. In counselling Val, I knew I was dealing with depression on a number of fronts, like fighting a war with the enemy coming from every side. Her situation drove me to pray more than I had with any other client in my career.

One day Val told me a story from her past. During her early years her father was in the armed forces. He was stationed overseas during this time. There was a great deal of tension between her father and mother, often resulting in verbal conflict and shouting. Her father's typical way of dealing with conflict was to leave the house. On many Friday evenings, he got drunk and would not come home again until Sunday evening. By Monday morning, he sobered up and was ready to go to work.

Val's family had two children, Val and her older brother. The brother was her mother's favourite; Val was her father's favourite. Because her parents were in constant tension with each other, they were drawn to their opposite-gender children in an 'illegal emotional attachment'. Whenever the father would go on weekend alcoholic binges, the mother would take her anger out on Val because she was her father's favourite. Thus, Val hated her father leaving. She not only missed her father, but also she faced her mother's angry tirades. Once, when Val was seven years old, her father angrily walked out of the house on a Friday evening and got into his car to drive away. Val ran after her father, crying, 'Daddy, Daddy, please don't leave me!' Tears filling her eyes, Val didn't notice where she was going. She ran straight into a tree. As her father was driving away from the curb, he happened to look in his rear-view mirror and saw what had happened to Val. He backed up, got out and picked her up, taking her into the house. Her nose was broken and her face was bloodied. As a result of her injuries, Val's father stayed home all weekend, looking after his daughter.

As she shared this story, I suddenly saw that the root of Val's depression was her anger toward her father. He always deserted her in her hour of need. At seven years old, Val learned that if she was in an injured state, her daddy would stay around and give her a daddy's love. A few years after this incident, her father was killed during a military training exercise. Val was left with unresolved anger toward her father, whom she idolized. She deeply grieved his loss. Of course, the anger between Val and her mother continued for years, with neither of them able to resolve ongoing tensions. Val's continuing codependent relationship with her mother was destructive to both of them.

When I first presented the possibility that the real anger fuelling her depression was toward her father, she questioned me vehemently. Val insisted she was angry with her mother, not her father. With the Holy Spirit's help I showed her that her father's desertion each weekend had left her vulnerable. His unfortunate and untimely death had left her permanently abandoned. She had never fully worked through her anger toward God (and her father). As we worked out this deeply buried anger toward her father using the Forgiveness Exercise (see Appendix 3), Val began changing dramatically. I learned a pivotal truth from the Holy Spirit (included in this book): the root of most, if not all, depression is unresolved anger and bitterness.

Cain and Abel

An interesting biblical illustration of this connection between anger and depression appears in Genesis 4 in the story of Cain and Abel:

> *Now Abel kept flocks, and Cain worked the soil. In the course of time Cain brought some of the fruits of the soil as an offering to the Lord. But Abel brought fat portions from some of the firstborn of his flock. The Lord looked with favour on Abel and his offering, but on Cain and his offering he did not look with favour. So Cain was very angry, and his face was downcast.*
>
> *Then the Lord said to Cain, 'Why are you angry? Why is your face downcast? If you do what is right, will you not be accepted? But if you do not do what is right, sin is crouching at your door; it desires to have you, but you must master it.'*

> *Now Cain said to his brother Abel, 'Let's go out to the field.' And while they were in the field, Cain attacked his brother Abel and killed him.*
>
> *(Genesis 4:2–8)*

There have been various interpretations to explain why Abel's sacrifice was acceptable to God and Cain's was not. My view is when the Lord clothed Adam and Eve with the skins of an animal, he communicated to them that animal sacrifice was a faith-picture necessary to understand how their sins were atoned for (looking forward to the ultimate sacrifice of Jesus on the cross). Although Cain knew what God expected, he chose to meet God on his own terms. We have been doing that ever since and it is called 'religion'.

When Cain's sacrifice was rejected, the Bible says he became very angry. The Hebrew uses the word *hara* to describe Cain's angry response. This word means 'to burn, to become hot in anger or to kindle a burning fire'. So Cain is described as burning with anger toward God. Being angry with the Almighty can be dangerous, so Cain expressed his anger inwardly instead of outwardly, yet his anger was revealed in his face. Verse 5 says 'his face was downcast'. What does this mean? It describes the state of depression, of anger turned inward. When the Lord confronted Cain with his angry response, he said to Cain, 'Why are you burning with anger and why has your face fallen?' (a literal translation from the Hebrew).

Cain was angry with God, with Abel, and with himself for failing to please God. Because Cain did not resolve his buried anger, the door opened to use the energy of his anger in a wrong way. He took his anger out on Abel, murdering him. Notice God's warning to Cain, before Cain killed Abel. God said to Cain, 'If you do what is right in the first place, you will not have to deal with rejection from me.

But if you do not deal with your sin properly and become angry in your rejection, you will leave yourself vulnerable to the power of sin and the power of the enemy looking to take advantage of you' (my paraphrase). Anger turned inward is no more acceptable than anger turned outward toward others. Unresolved or buried anger is destructive, no matter how it is expressed. God said to Cain, 'You must master it [i.e. sin], or it will master you' (literal Hebrew translation). We cannot leave depression untreated, or it ultimately will destroy us.

Suicide

Depression left untreated can lead to suicide. Suicide is the potential outcome for people who turn their anger inward. When they demean themselves, destroying their worth and value, then nothing may stop them from killing themselves. Suicide results when individuals see no hope for change in their present situation. Suicidal people reason that living is pointless because they view themselves as useless and worthless.

This downward spiral of anger turned inward, leading to depression and ultimately to suicide, can be seen in the story of Jonah. Jonah's life is an interesting study in depression and potential suicide. Asked by God to preach repentance to his hated enemy, Assyria, Jonah chose to run away rather than obey God. For a man who was used to hearing the voice of God, he wasn't thinking clearly when he made that decision. Really, how can you run from the omnipresent, Almighty God? But we run away all the time, don't we? So maybe we should empathize with Jonah's stupidity a little. After God had rescued Jonah from his watery grave and errant fishing expedition, he agreed to obey God.

I'm not quite sure why Jonah disobeyed God in the first place, but perhaps he had a suspicion that the mercy of God would outweigh the judgment of God. Jonah was commanded by God to 'preach against it [Nineveh], because its wickedness has come up before me' (Jonah 1:2). So Jonah reluctantly agreed to journey to Nineveh. But, hey, what better message to tell an enemy you hate, than that God is going to destroy them? Perhaps what caught Jonah off guard was that the Ninevites believed God, from the lowliest servant to the king himself. A fast was proclaimed, repentance was expressed and God removed his threatened destruction from the nation. Hallelujah! Revival came to a whole godless nation, almost overnight.

Come on now, Jonah – this outcome is something to get excited about! However, Jonah was not pleased at all. Like Cain, he 'burned with anger' (literal translation from the Hebrew). Assyria was Israel's national enemy. Jonah felt angry that his enemy had repented, thus avoiding God's wrath. In his anger, Jonah asked God to kill him. Not suicide by lethal injection, but suicide by 'divine injection'. How many of us have been so angry with God and with ourselves that we have also asked God to take our lives?

Then God asked a penetrating question of Jonah: 'Have you any right to be burning with anger?' (my paraphrase). Anger was given to us to defend ourselves and others from danger. Jonah perceived Assyria as Israel's deadly enemy, forgetting that no enemy is stronger than God. When we fear God, we don't have to fear anything or anyone else. If Jonah had used his anger for energy to preach against the enemy of their souls (Satan), he would have used his anger as God intended. But his unforgiveness toward the Assyrians allowed the enemy of his soul to turn the anger both outward toward the Ninevites and inward toward himself. Jonah's depression and desire for suicide was the result of buried anger that he had not worked out through forgiveness and repentance.

Chapter 5
How Anger Affects Your Body

Anger expressed in the body (psychosomatic illnesses)

The second way in which anger can be expressed inwardly is toward the body. Psychosomatic illnesses and diseases in the body are caused by emotional issues and/or mental attitudes that have not been properly healed (*psycho* is to do with the mind and *soma* is to do with the body). Notice that I am not saying that all physical illnesses are the result of unhealed emotional wounds. There is still a great deal of debate among professionals about the effects that emotional states can have on the physical body. Psychoneuro-immunological research (interactions of the mind and body – how stress transforms into disease) is a relatively new field of research in the medical community that is finding a growing following among some investigators. However, as a psychologist (and pastor), I remain alert to the possible root of unresolved bitterness as a source of psychosomatic illnesses. Today, psychoneuro-immunological research explores the relationship between mind and body in the context of health and wellness. The research proposes that negative stress undermines the immune system by releasing higher cortisol levels in the body. A search on the internet reveals numerous studies which link anger and heart disease. Let's examine a number of these common physical disorders in the context of anger turned inward.

Tension headaches

Tension headaches are an example of psychosomatic illness. Continual headaches could arise from a physiological problem, a structural problem, an abnormality in the brain itself, or a problem in the chemistry of the brain, among others. But it is also possible that the headaches are caused by internalized stress, which comes from buried anger and unforgiveness. If someone were to come to me for counselling and report that he is having continuous headaches, I would encourage him to check for all physical possibilities. If the problem is not resolved medically, the person should consider unresolved anger as a root issue. The anger stored in one's body causes muscles to tense. Constant tension in the muscles and bone structure can lead to headaches. The tense muscles in the back of the neck create inflammation through traction on the skull, resulting in pain.

Migraine headaches

Migraine headaches are another example of psychosomatic illness. Migraines are caused by changes in brain chemistry. These are vascular disturbances, a constriction and expansion of the blood vessels in the brain, which sometimes are related to food substances. Admittedly, migraines are difficult and complex. Anyone struggling with this type of headache does not need someone's pat answers. However, I often ask: Do migraine headaches correlate with buried anger? When we store anger, we eventually change our brain chemistry. Anger which has accumulated over a lengthy period of time could contribute to a change in brain chemistry. Could this change in chemistry lead to migraine headaches? It is worth checking.

Ulcers

Ulcers are also considered to be psychosomatic. The hormones associated with excessive stress and buried anger are known to cause acid production in the stomach (i.e. the small intestine). The accumulation of hydrochloric acid in the stomach (duodenal ulcers) can eventually cause destruction of the lining of the stomach. The resulting pain of bleeding ulcers attests to the destructive nature of stored anger.

Crohn's disease and ulcerative colitis

Ulcerative colitis and Crohn's disease are the two most common forms of inflammatory bowel disease. These conditions cause chronic inflammation of the digestive tract, which is painful and debilitating. Ulcerative colitis and Crohn's disease are so similar that they can be mistaken for each other. Both cause severe bouts of watery diarrhoea and abdominal pain due to inflammation in the digestive tract. These symptoms often are accompanied by fever, loss of appetite, and weight loss. Crohn's disease occurs anywhere in the digestive tract, spreading to other layers of affected tissues. Ulcerative colitis, on the other hand, usually affects the lining of the large intestine (i.e. the colon) and the rectum.

There is no consensus on the causes of ulcerative colitis and Crohn's. Some believe they are caused by a virus or bacteria that the immune system is fighting. Others think it may be related to heredity or a gene connection. Still others think it may be caused by environmental factors, such as a high-fat diet or too many refined foods, or living in industrialized nations. Certainly, ulcerative colitis and Crohn's are exacerbated by stress and the pressures of life. Stored anger definitely hinders fighting these conditions.

High blood pressure

Hypertension or high blood pressure, leading to heart attacks, can relate to uncontrolled stress or anger. Of course, not all high blood pressure is caused by mishandled anger, but too often the accumulated effects of a lifestyle of anger wrongly expressed can lead to heart attacks.

Jack, a bitter man, used his anger to control people. He headed a company that employed over 100 people. His company was successful financially because he was a driven man. At the age of forty-five, he had a small fortune and could do anything he wanted. However, as a cynic, he distrusted everyone, especially his employees. As a result he often double-checked their work. This would lead to conflict with his managers and angry outbursts in the office. Unfortunately, he proudly believed that his success was due to his drive and his fiery temper. Although he remained married, his wife led a life of her own, avoiding his company whenever possible. His two grown children also wanted little to do with him because of his many outbursts.

One afternoon, while he was rushing back to work in his car, another motorist cut him off. His usual reaction was to lean on the horn and speed up 'to pay the jerk back'. But, suddenly, he felt a pain like a red-hot poker pushed through his chest. He managed to drive to the nearest hospital where he was checked for a heart attack.

Over the next few days, the tests showed no indication

of a heart attack. When he even passed a stress test, the doctors ordered one final blood test. The lab technician had difficulty finding a vein; by the fourth try, Jack was incensed. The 'red-hot poker' struck again. As a result, further tests were ordered, which showed that one of his coronary arteries was almost completely blocked. When he expressed rage, his heart failed to receive the blood it required, sending a pain signal to warn him. This man's out-of-control anger was in danger of killing him, literally.

Type-A personalities

Research by two pioneering cardiologists, Meyer Friedman and Ray Rosenman, in the 1970s, suggested that 'Type-A people' are more heart-attack prone. They described Type-A personalities as hard-driving, ambitious, competitive, impatient and easily moved toward hostility and rage. Their research showed that when people explode with rage, their bodies produce an outpouring of adrenaline and other stress hormones, causing certain physical effects. The voice changes to a higher pitch and the rate and depth of breathing increases. The heart beats faster and harder, and the arm and leg muscles tighten. They feel 'charged up' and ready for action. The cumulative effect of hormones released during these anger episodes can increase the risk of coronary and related diseases.

Further research done by Friedman and Rosenman indicated that Type A's could significantly reduce their danger of heart attacks by changing their diet and exercise habits and by getting counselling to change their attitudes toward how they handled their anger. Assessments made after four and a half years showed that the group receiving both cardiac and behavioural counselling had decreased the dangerous Type-A behaviour by a substantial degree. People in the comparison group had decreased their Type-A behaviour only to a limited extent. More importantly, a 45 per cent reduction in the rate of recurrent heart problems and mortality rates developed among those who modified their behaviour. Reducing dangerous anger expression is one way to prevent both a first heart attack and a subsequent one.

Cancer

Increasingly, research suggests that cancer may be caused by the break-down of the immune system. Over a long period of time, stored anger or bitterness can lead to the inability of the immune system to fight the attack from cancer cells in the body.

Sylvia had bone cancer in her early twenties. She was a kind woman with a gentle disposition. Her parents taught her that being passive was an honourable feminine quality. As a result, she received enormous hurt, particularly from her husband, who was dominant and aggressive. Instead of using her anger to confront her husband, she stored it; eventually she became vulnerable to the attack from cancer. When she finally agreed to counselling, Sylvia had a difficult time expressing her deep anger toward her husband. She continually blamed herself for the troubles in their marriage. When it was suggested to her that her husband's sexual treatment of her was abusive, she sobbed and the pain poured out. Agreeing to write out her anger, she wrote volumes, realizing how much anger was inside. Sylvia could not see she was such an angry person because her anger was internalized. There was no way to medically 'prove' that her cancer was caused by internalized anger. But the breakdown of her immune system and the resulting cancer in her body correlated with the extent of the stored anger in her body. It was not likely to be a coincidence.

Anorexia and bulimia

In psychological literature, anorexia and bulimia are considered self-esteem issues. Indeed they are! But also I see them as issues that have a 'root' of anger. An anorexic or bulimic person is saying, 'I don't like my body size or shape; I am going to starve it or binge it to try to keep it slim and trim.' How a girl or woman feels about her own body is an issue of acceptance. In essence, she is saying, 'I don't like myself as I am; I am angry enough at myself or others to starve my body.' When working with anger as the basis of eating disorders, rather than treating the symptoms of the anorexia or bulimia, I have enjoyed considerable success. Often, the cause of anorexia or bulimia is anger within the family system, which previously was not addressed.

Overeating

In the same way, overeating can also be an expression of anger against the body. Just as in the case of starving or purging, the overeater is saying, 'I don't care about myself, so why should I take care of my body?' Obviously, people who struggle with overeating don't consciously say to themselves, 'I'm angry with myself.' In truth, they are saying, 'I don't like myself, I don't like the things I do, I don't like the way I behave, so why should I take care of my body? It simply doesn't matter.' A number of reasons cause people to overeat, so we can't blame it all on buried anger. Overeaters overeat because they like the taste of food, and they lack self-control. But internalized anger is often a contributing factor. We should examine unresolved anger in our past lives. That process may well reveal some clues as to overcoming our battle with food.

Structural problems

Stored anger also contributes to conditions such as backaches, neck problems and jaw problems. Clearly, these physical problems have numerous causes, but when no explanation can be given for the symptoms, then one should examine buried anger as a possible root. Can you recall the tension you have felt in your body after you have had an explosion of rage at someone? Tension in the muscles often results from unresolved tensions in our emotions. If you have stress-filled encounters with colleagues, supervisors, customers or clients at work, you can feel tension in your neck, shoulders and back as you drive home. Just think of the times you stored anger over the years and then calculate the amount of tension your body must have absorbed from the buried anger.

Chapter 6

Learning to Use Anger for Good

Making anger work for you

Every violation of our personhood releases anger in us, automatically. Any time we are hurt, in any way, the 'anger button' goes off automatically. It is the way God has designed us. What happens to that anger energy in our bodies? Anger energy, once produced, does not disappear into thin air. It stays in our bodies until it is used as energy in some other form. Because we do not like to acknowledge we are angry, we repress the anger and consequently store the anger energy. When we do not acknowledge our anger consciously, we become unable to use anger for its intended purpose. If, instead, we use our awareness of anger as a means to explore danger to us, then we can use anger expression as a signal to explore what is going on inside of us. Then we can use our anger as a means of discovering the violation against us. Where have we been hurt? Whom do we need to forgive? How can we release hurt or anger to God for his solution to our pain?

Anger as preparedness and power

Anger, as energy, prepares you to deal with danger. God has also given anger to you as a warning. When you sense danger, the fear signal will alert you to that possibility. There are three types of danger – real, potential and perceived. If a snarling dog is attacking you, and you have no way to defend yourself, you are facing real danger. Assuming your fear of the dog does not overwhelm you, leaving you paralysed, the anger energy will enable you to fight the dog or run, whatever may be wisest. Potential danger is that same dog, behind a rickety fence, charging you, and trying to get through or over the fence. The danger is not immediate, but if that snarling dog gets outside of the fence, you are in real danger.

The problem of perceived danger

However, perceived danger is the type of danger that creates the most difficulty. When you think the danger is real, you act as if it were. Because it is real to you, you respond to that danger as if it were genuine but, of course, it is not real danger. When you do not interpret the danger correctly, you will act inappropriately with your anger energy. Real danger will produce the energy of anger, which you need to help you deal with the danger. Potential danger should do the same in you. But in perceived danger, the anger energy prepares your body to protect you from something not real.

A husband and wife had come to see me for some marriage issues. The husband's job required him to travel frequently, which caused tension in the marriage. The wife was concerned because she sensed her husband was having an adulterous affair while away on business. Whenever he came back from his trips she would grill him endlessly because she sensed danger to their marriage. He reacted with defensiveness to her accusations, which confirmed her assumptions. So when I saw the husband alone, I confronted him about his wife's accusations, and he swore on a 'stack of Bibles' that he was faithful to his wife.

In the final outcome, he had been truthful. He had been worried about their financial situation and his ability to pay their bills. Because of his concerns about the money, he became emotionally distant. As a result of his stress and his wife's anger, he lacked interest in making love to her. This led his wife to think that he was having an affair. Her anger was misdirected and misused because she believed her husband was unfaithful. In fact, this man loved his wife very much but hated his job. His job took him away from home too much. As a result of counselling, he changed jobs after realizing how destructive the travels were to their marriage.

Anger empowers us to face danger

Anger empowers us to act against danger. Often fear holds us back from dealing with danger we sense. Anger energy empowers us to resolve the danger, despite the fear. Just suppose you are having conflict with your boss at work. The boss has the potential to fire you, or give you a poor evaluation, which would affect your next pay rise. How do you get the courage honestly to tell your boss about your feelings concerning the conflict between you and him? Most likely, you will not confront the boss until you get in touch with your anger. Your anger energizes you to speak truthfully. Anger prepares and empowers you to face what is danger to you; or, perhaps what you perceive as danger.

I experienced this very employer–employee conflict in the first year I worked at a local community college as a counsellor. My first day on the job was registration day for the students. I was not only new to the college, but also new to the city. Some new students knew more about the college than I did! Yet I was expected give them directions in regard to their classes and schedules. When I volunteered to work a week early to 'learn the ropes', my boss said it was unnecessary. (I think they were trying to save money by not having me do an extra week's work.) So, when I gave wrong advice to a student on my first day, one of the instructors heard about it. He angrily told my dean about my mistake. My dean took me into his office, closed the door and tore into me. His use of strong language was both an over-reaction and abusive.

The unfairness caused anger to rise up in me. Even though I was not an outgoing or assertive type of person at that time, something rose up inside of me. I said to my dean, 'I don't think I deserve this kind of verbal abuse from you.' I had only been on the job for two days and yet here I was, confronting the boss. I told him angrily, 'It was you who said I didn't need to come in a week early, even when I had offered to do so. If I made a mistake, I would be glad to talk with the instructor and get things sorted out, but I don't think it is right of you to treat me in this manner.' What caused my response? Anger! Anger energized me to overcome my fear and speak the truth to my superior. Two years later, when my dean was leaving the college, I attended his farewell party. As he said goodbye, he recalled that incident in his office. He told my wife and me that he had respected me from that day because of my willingness to stand up for myself properly. However, I realize that if I used anger in a wrong way to demean him and to retaliate for his anger toward me, I would have lost the value of the energy that the anger was providing (maybe I would have lost my job too!).

A biblical example

In Nehemiah 5 we find this story:

> *Now the men and their wives raised a great outcry against*
> *their Jewish brothers. Some were saying, 'We and our*
> *sons and daughters are numerous; in order for us to eat*
> *and stay alive, we must get grain.' Others were saying,*
> *'We are mortgaging our fields, our vineyards and our*
> *homes to get grain during the famine.' Still others were*
> *saying, 'We have had to borrow money to pay the king's*
> *tax on our fields and vineyards. Although we are of the*
> *same flesh and blood as our countrymen and though our*
> *sons are as good as theirs, yet we have to subject our sons*
> *and daughters to slavery. Some of our daughters have*
> *already been enslaved, but we are powerless, because our*
> *fields and our vineyards belong to others.'*
>
> *When I heard their outcry and these charges, I was*
> *very angry. I pondered them in my mind and then*
> *accused the nobles and officials. I told them, 'You are*
> *exacting usury from your own countrymen!' So I called*
> *together a large meeting to deal with them and said: 'As*
> *far as possible, we have bought back our Jewish brothers*
> *who were sold to the Gentiles. Now you are selling your*
> *brothers, only for them to be sold back to us!' They kept*
> *quiet, because they could find nothing to say.*
>
> *(Nehemiah 5:1–8)*

Here were some Jewish people treating their own countrymen with contempt by charging them exorbitant interest on the money they had loaned them. The interest rate was so high that these Jewish brothers found it necessary to sell their sons and daughters into slavery, just to pay the interest. When Nehemiah heard of the injustice, an angry response rose in him. This is power with a purpose. Nehemiah, using his anger, confronted the leaders of the business community with their wrong. By so doing, he set wrongs right and prevented the enemy from destroying God's people from within their own ranks. Nehemiah used the power of anger correctly.

Chapter 7

Choosing How to Use Your Anger

The power of anger

My parents raised six children. My siblings include an older sister named Judy, a twin brother named Grant, a younger brother named Ross and twin sisters, Lynne and Elaine. There were six children in six years, including two sets of twins. My parents were very busy! As brothers growing up, we were good friends, but we sometimes fought. Grant and I were evenly matched because we were the same age and size. But our younger brother, Ross, was no match for us because he was younger and smaller (that is, until he got older). When he was younger, he didn't have a chance in most of our physical contests. However, when, on occasion, he got very angry, we learned the power of anger. It was like getting between a mother bear and her cubs. Not a good idea!

We have a choice

How we use the power of anger's energy is a choice. We could use anger to rage and control others. Or, for example, we can use anger's energy passively, to pout. On the other hand, we could direct the energy of our anger inward and attack ourselves for being 'so stupid'. Alternatively, we could store the anger, allowing it to slowly destroy our immune systems. However, we also could use the anger energy to confront the danger in a constructive way. In other words, we all can learn to develop strategies to deal effectively with problems. The choice is ours. But to do this we need a fundamental shift from viewing anger as bad, to seeing anger as good. God gave us anger for our benefit. The difference is contrasted between the way King Saul used his anger and the way David used anger. Saul used anger to defend his insecure personality by trying to kill David. David used his anger for good, to kill Goliath, giving the Israelite army a great victory.

Anger as control

Sometimes anger is used to help us put control back into our lives when we feel out of control. When anger remains buried and we are unaware of its presence, it will express itself in ways we are not conscious of. In that way, while anger is used to control others, we are not in control of it ourselves. Often we feel badly about our inability to control the expressions of our anger. Clearly, we want control of our anger, because God has given it to us for our good. The more insecure we feel, the more vulnerable we become to expressing anger inappropriately. For example, when my children are ignoring me, I feel out of control as a parent. Too many times, I have used anger to control my children. Anger used as energy will certainly get control back. There is no question about that. Parents often use inappropriately expressed anger to restrain their children, because they think they need it. Unfortunately, it brings short-term results but long-term consequences – alienation from their children. When we use anger as control wrongly, we alienate other people from us as well.

A mother and son came for counselling. The son was performing poorly in school. The mother felt it was because the father often exploded in anger at the son. The father, who worked for the government, was constantly hearing rumours about job cuts in his department. Every time he heard the rumours, he became insecure. He would return from his work, expressing his anger toward his family, particularly his son. The son reacted by turning his anger inward. Depressed, the son had little energy left for studying. When the boy's father finally agreed to counselling, he revealed that he had acted much the same way as a boy. The grandfather was a farmer. He was under constant financial pressure because much depended upon a good crop year. When the grandfather felt insecure about farm finances, he aimed his anger at the family. Accordingly, the father repeated the same cycle of anger expression that he had grown up with.

Who's in charge?

Whenever we successfully use anger to control others, we conclude that anger works to subdue those who oppose us. Perhaps you have heard the phrase, 'We don't lose our tempers, we use our tempers.' However, anger should not control us – we should control it. To control anger, we must understand the root of buried anger. Proverbs 29:11 says, 'The fool gives full vent to his anger, but the wise man keeps himself under control.' Psalm 14 reminds us that the fool is one who says there is no God. The fool is not always an atheist or an agnostic. The fool is a person who functions as if God is not actively present in his life. The fool takes control of his circumstances by using anger as rage, because he doesn't believe that God is in charge of his circumstances. The wise man, on the other hand, is aware of God's presence, and acts accordingly by controlling himself. He believes that God is in charge; therefore he doesn't express his anger as rage to take control.

On one of my trips to India, I arrived at the Mumbai airport only to discover that one of my suitcases had not arrived – the one which contained my seminar materials. Airline agents traced the suitcase and it was put on another airplane arriving in Mumbai early the next morning. They advised me to retrieve it at 7 a.m. the next day. I was annoyed at the inconvenience, but decided not to use my anger wrongfully by expressing annoyance. Up at five the next morning, I arrived at the airport only to discover that Customs would not release my suitcase until an agent from the other airline had signed the proper documents. Oh, the joys of Indian bureaucracy!

The trouble was, I was scheduled to do a seminar on the other side of the city, and it would take an hour and a half to travel there by taxi. Nothing moves fast in Mumbai airports or traffic. I knew I was angry about this unnecessary delay, but I prayed, asking the Lord what was going on. I realized I was under attack from spiritual forces, but I knew God was still in charge. I felt anger rising within me but I also knew the futility of expressing my anger to get action. I needed to turn that anger into prayer, and I did so.

Although I was an hour late for the seminar, God prepared the way for me. I had planned to begin the seminar with worship, as the Lord's presence was crucial for the success of our seminar on 'Overcoming Addictions'. Arriving at the church building, I discovered that the pastor had played a worship video while they were waiting; the people were wonderfully prepared! The presence of the Lord was obvious in the seminar. Turning my anger into prayer allowed God to take care of things much better than my anger would have. Incidentally, the ticket agent who helped retrieve my suitcase was working the day I returned to the airport to leave Mumbai some two weeks later. She remembered me, and the hassle I had been through. She blessed me wonderfully by upgrading me into business class. God is very much in charge!

Anger is like dynamite. Put in the hands of a construction foreman who knows how to work with it, dynamite becomes a useful tool for the construction of the highway project. However, in the hands of a fool, dynamite is a dangerous and destructive weapon. Remember Proverbs 29:11: 'A fool gives full vent to his anger, but a wise man keeps himself under control.'

Burying anger is the worst way to deal with it

The most common way of dealing with anger, in every culture I have been in, is to repress it or bury it. The process of burying anger occurs consciously or unconsciously. Technically, the conscious process of burying anger is called suppression; the unconscious process is known as repression. More anger is buried unconsciously than consciously. Because we feel ashamed or guilty about our anger expression, we bury feelings of anger. We bury anger because we believe anger is negative and destructive, or because we fear anger and its impact on our relationships.

Sometimes, we repress anger because we misunderstand it – it confuses us. Repression attempts to control the energy of anger by pushing it out of our conscious minds. Sometimes, we even deny we are angry, when we are aware of the anger we are feeling. Other times, we deny we are angry because we don't think we are angry. Like children, we reason that if we are not thinking about it, it doesn't exist. If we are unaware of something, it can't be happening. But by pushing something out of our conscious minds, we lose control of it. Although we are no longer aware of it, anger is still operating in us, but outside of our control. At other times, we repress anger unconsciously, because we have trained ourselves to do so. Either way, burying anger is the worst way of dealing with it.

Dealing with the anger of the past

A couple came for counselling to resolve problems in their marriage. Listening to the initial presentation of their anger toward each other, the counsellor saw quickly that each carried a distorted perspective of the other. The husband, George, came from a family where his father was highly involved with his career. As a result, George's mother was not cared for emotionally, nor was George. The mother's emotional needs were met through her son, and as a result, George had become dependent upon his mother for his identity and security. George was the epitome of masculinity in his looks and body build. He was all man. But emotionally, George was more feminine in his outlook.

When George sought a mate, he looked for a woman who had strength of character. He had come to believe that to function as a man, he needed a strong woman to rely on. He had learned this notion from his family system. George's father's partial success in his family life was due to George's mother being the quiet strength of the family. However, his mother developed significant buried anger because her husband neglected her. Although George needed his mother, he also resented her because, deep inside, he felt inadequate as a man. He depended on his mother for strength. When George met Janice, he was sure she was suited to him. Although Janice was more outgoing than George's mother, she had the same strength of character as his mother. Unknowingly, this was one of the key characteristics that drew George to marry Janice.

Janice came from a family in which her father had little respect for women. Although a good provider, he was constantly critical of his wife and his three daughters. Because of her father's demeaning attitude toward women, Janice made this unconscious vow in her mind: 'I'll never marry a man like my father. I will marry a man whom I can control.' She wanted a masculine-looking man, but one having little strength of character. When Janice met George, they seemed like the north and south poles of a magnet. The attraction was instant; but neither knew their motivation for marrying. Years later, when George withdrew more and more from the relationship to pursue his career, Janice tried everything she could think of to get things back under control. Yet the more she tried to control the relationship and her husband, the more he resisted and pulled away.

Both George and Janice, in harbouring unrealized anger toward their parents, distorted their attitudes toward each other. As the counsellor began working with them, he saw them separately to deal with the buried anger from their families of origin. This approach allowed them to see their difficulty in trusting each other in the marriage relationship. George was similar to Janice's dad; Janice was like George's mother. The buried anger from their growing-up years made it difficult for either of them to trust that the other would change. A lot of hard work was required to untangle what they had brought into the marriage.

Part 2

Turning Anger into a Friend

Chapter 8

Steps to Using Anger for Your Good

Until now, I have examined anger through its definition, 'energy given to us by God to protect us from danger'. We have seen that the mishandling of anger expression creates problems in our lives. It is not the anger itself that is the problem. We have also noted that many daily issues that we face are rooted in stored anger. It bears repeating again: anger is not bad, it is good. Anger is designed by God to give us a way of dealing effectively with the potential danger around us. But although managing our anger expression is important, when we fail to deal with the root, we only treat the symptoms, and we bury a great amount of anger energy. So, to treat anger issues effectively, we must do both. We must examine the stored anger, as well as deal with how we express our anger in the present.

The big black cauldron

For now, however, we want to shift our focus from anger as the root, to the question of managing the way we express anger. In psychology, the term commonly used is 'anger management', a necessary part of dealing with anger. I want to provide an analogy that shows how anger as a root issue and anger management work together. Picture in your mind a large black cauldron, a big black pot. This cauldron represents all the stored hurt and anger you have from the experiences of life. At some point in your life, based on how much hurt and pain you have suffered, this big black pot fills and begins overflowing.

When anger overflows the 'big black cauldron', you express anger in unacceptable ways. You may rage at someone, or withdraw from a close relationship, or get into a depressed state, or perhaps you will develop physical symptoms that cause concern. Finally, you decide you need help with your life. Because life is not going well, you realize you can't handle problems by yourself any more. When you finally make that appointment to see a counsellor, he or she recognizes that your anger is telling you that you need to manage your anger. The counsellor releases the emotional pressure you are under by listening to you, giving you good advice for your situation. In other words, he or she takes a 'scoop or two' off the top of your 'overflowing cauldron'. You feel much better, at least for the moment. The level of your anger energy goes down and you feel like you can handle life again. The counselling has worked and you continue with life. However, before long, the stresses and conflicts catch up with you. The 'big black pot' gets filled up again.

Remembering the counsellor, you return for more help. The counsellor enables you to see where you are handling things wrongly, and you feel better again. A few more scoops are taken off the top of your 'big black cauldron'. When the level of stored anger declines, you feel better. But sooner or later, stress causes more anger and your pot overflows again. The third time you visit your counsellor, you wonder if counselling helps at all. Nothing seems to be changing and you are making the same mistakes repeatedly. What needs to be done?

Quite honestly, the only way to deal effectively with

this overflowing cauldron of anger in your life is to place a tap in the bottom of the pot to drain the buried anger. Anger management is like 'scooping' anger off the top. In the long run, anger management is ineffective unless the pot is first drained from the bottom. Part 1 of this book dealt with how the anger cauldron filled initially. Part 2 deals with the skills that are necessary for the daily management of the pressures that trigger anger responses in us. In Part 3 I will show how to use forgiveness to drain the 'anger cauldron' through a tap in the bottom.

The value of anger management

Although we are now shifting our focus to anger management, I want to emphasize the importance of always dealing with the buried anger. The next few chapters provide practical guidelines for dealing with daily anger issues in life. Hopefully these hands-on, logical steps will provide the 'how-to's' of handling anger issues. These chapters show how to turn anger into a friend instead of an enemy. Let's examine these helpful steps in resolving present issues of anger:

- Step 1: Learn to recognize the 'anger button'.
- Step 2: Think back through the causes of your anger.
- Step 3: Get in control of your anger.
- Step 4: Use anger's power to motivate.
- Step 5: Deal with the shame of anger.

Step 1: Learn to recognize the 'anger button'

The first step in turning anger into a friend is learning to pay attention to the 'anger button'. Obviously no actual 'anger button' exists on the human body, but the analogy helps us understand what is going on inside of us. In managing anger effectively, we must recognize our anger. Because we have been well trained to bury our anger unconsciously, we must retrain for awareness of the anger. We have all had occasions when we felt anger inside but we denied that we were angry. As a result, we have repressed the anger.

The first step in effectively resolving anger is to become aware when the 'anger button' goes off. Denial is one of our primary defence mechanisms in controlling anger. To aid us in this denial process, we use euphemisms. Euphemisms are nice sayings or inoffensive expressions that avoid more offensive expressions. We use euphemisms to replace other terms that seem frightening or disgusting.

For example, euphemisms are commonly used in dealing with the subject of death. We don't like saying a person has died. It seems too harsh, too stark. So we say, 'He passed away' or 'He has gone to meet his Maker'. Sometimes, in a more crass way, we say, 'He kicked the bucket'. We use euphemisms when we are uncomfortable discussing sexual parts of our bodies. A set of slang words has developed because we don't like to use words like 'penis' or 'vagina'. Strangely enough, we react in the same way with anger. We don't like to think of ourselves as angry, or expressing anger. Generally we perceive anger as bad and shameful.

Examples of euphemisms

Let me provide some examples. Rather than admitting our anger, we say we are 'ticked off'. By avoiding the use of the word 'angry', we deny our anger. Because we think of anger as rage – that is, 'blowing our stack' (another euphemism) – we think that being 'ticked off' is not really anger. It is medium-level anger and, therefore, not full-blown anger. As we see, anger expression is released at various levels. Low-level anger is what we commonly call frustration. So we say, 'I'm not angry. I'm a little frustrated.' In so doing we deny our anger. The accumulation of many experiences of frustration can eventually lead us to explode in rage later. My reason for calling frustration low-grade anger is to identify it as anger. We need to honestly face our anger. The word 'frustration' is descriptive, but let's use it in a manner that allows us to acknowledge that we are angry. Instead of saying, 'I'm frustrated', we should say, 'I'm a little angry.' Then we would become aware that the 'anger button' has been triggered.

Here is another euphemistic expression that is commonly used: 'Yes, I was a little disappointed, but I will get over it.' Disappointment means that somebody did not meet our expectations. The 'anger button' went off even though we may be unaware of it. Although it may be low-grade anger, nevertheless the energy of anger has been released into our bodies and minds because we were hurt by someone disappointing us. Or we may say, 'I was bothered by it, but it's not a big deal. I'm mature enough to handle it.' The anger button signalled us but we did not notice it because of the words we used. However, when we meet the person who 'bothered' us, we may try to avoid that person because of our low-level anger.

Perhaps we say, 'Yes, I was hurt by him, but I can handle it.' In using this expression, we have dismissed the fact that we are angry because we are hurt. All hurt is danger to us, so the 'anger button' automatically will go off when we hurt. This is the way God has created us. Another expression we often use: 'Yeah, it bugs me a little when she treats me that way, but that's just the way she is.' Again, we have dismissed our anger because we think we should tolerate someone who 'bugs' us. Or, we use the expression, 'I'm a little annoyed' or 'I'm a trifle upset'. All these euphemisms hide the fact that the energy of anger has been released in our bodies; yet we are not aware of it. I am not being technical or splitting hairs here. I am alerting us to be aware that the 'anger button' has gone off. We need training to deal with anger properly.

Feeling anger in your body

Here are some other ways to raise awareness of our anger. You can feel anger in your body. For example, you are in a conversation with someone, and he or she says something unkind or puts in a little 'dig'. Or, perhaps the comment is not meant unkindly, but nevertheless it hits you right in your heart. Immediately, you feel tightness in your chest or your muscles. You are vaguely aware that something has gone off in you but you have not defined it. Some time later, when you have time to think about their comment, you realize you were hurt.

Or, at the end of a busy day, you develop a tension headache. Perhaps it resulted from the busyness at work or from the pace of the day. But the headache may also result from several tension-filled issues from the day, resulting in low-level anger accumulating in your body. The tension headache could signal to you that you have been harbouring low-grade anger all day. Backaches, neck tension or even jaw tension may all signal that you are carrying stress from unresolved anger. Emotions act as signals. What you 'feel' in your body, you need to investigate. Pain works the same way. When you feel pain in your body, it is the body's way of signalling that something is wrong that needs checking.

Relationships can signal anger

The state of our relationships also exposes the presence

of anger. Think of a close relationship with someone. You notice that distance has crept into your friendship. That's a clue that anger may have developed in your relationship, even though you hadn't noticed. I have found that unnoticed anger is common in marriages, including my own. Amid the busyness of life, you notice that your spouse has not been warm or affectionate lately. It doesn't have to arise from a major blow-up. It can be a small incident that has resulted in one of you pulling away from the other. Or, you think, 'I should phone my friend. We haven't talked in a few days.' But you hesitate, and think, 'I won't call after all.' Could this be a signal that anger has crept into the relationship, creating emotional distance? We need to pay attention to the signals we sense through emotional distance.

Feeling down?

Sometimes, the signal in us can best be described as a 'down' feeling. You come home from work or the office at the end of the day feeling low, without any immediate explanation for this feeling. When you take time to examine this feeling, it may indicate that anger has accumulated in you. You have been too busy or stressed to notice. It isn't until you have time to be alone that you notice this feeling. It doesn't matter how mature you are, or how 'spiritual' you are, the hurts of life produce anger automatically. You need to recognize your 'anger button' going off. This is the first step in beginning to use anger for good, rather than accumulating anger as a destructive force.

Chapter 9

Paying Attention to the Anger Signal

Step 2: Think back through the causes of your anger

Step 1 is becoming aware that your 'anger button' has been triggered. Step 2 is discovering what the 'anger button' is signalling. The 'anger button' always goes off for a reason. Even when the reason is invalid to others, it is valid to you. When the 'anger button' triggers, it means you sensed danger. The anger energy aroused in you prepares a defence. The question you need to be asking is: What is the danger I am sensing? Remember, there are three types of danger: real, potential and perceived. Was the 'anger button' signalling real danger? If the danger is bluntly obvious, you are aware of it and the energy of anger will aid you. Potential danger is less obvious. For example, an unkind comment to you can signal the anger that a friend has toward you. Or, perhaps the boss said something to you as you were leaving work, indicating that he is unhappy with your recent performance. It was not a direct comment but a subtle one that indicates his disappointment with some of your work. You sense anger in your emotions over his comment. The potential danger of conflict with the boss needs evaluating.

Perceived danger is usually the most difficult to

determine. Even though you perceive danger to yourself, it may not be real danger. But because you perceive it as danger, it will signal you in the same way as real danger. Ask yourself, is real danger approaching or am I reacting to unresolved issues in my life? Is something from your background causing an over-reaction to another's comment? Your friend or colleague may have meant the comment as a compliment, but you took it the wrong way because of some unresolved sensitive issue in your past. Later, you find that he or she meant something entirely different. Your reaction explains that there is something going on inside you. When you have been alerted by the emotional signal of anger, you can use your mind to process the feelings that you have observed. You can ask yourself, why did the 'anger button' go off?

Let me share a personal example of this. After nine years of working as a counsellor at Lethbridge Community College, I applied for and received a teaching position in the psychology department. The first year of teaching was a survival year. Not only did I have to learn to teach classes day after day, but also I had to develop the teaching curriculum, tests and audio-visuals that I used. At times my preparation was only one week ahead of the students. As an inexperienced teacher, I was more than a little insecure. I worked about twelve hours a day, six days a week to keep up. Besides the teaching, I also pastored our small church. It was a very busy, stretching time. The second semester of that first year, I taught a class in psychology to criminal justice students (future police officers). They were a challenge to teach because most of them were not enamoured with studying psychology.

After the first class of the day, a student spoke with me. We were about a month into the semester, so I would have delivered several lectures. The students would have written two tests by this time. The student was angry with me and bluntly told me what he thought of both my class and my teaching. Being insecure myself, I dismissed the anger as his problem. Other students wanted to see me after class as well. As I had another class right away, I had no time to process this student's angry tirade. I went on with my day, forgetting about the incident. Or, so I thought.

At the end of the day, as I was leaving the college buildings, walking to my car, I had a 'down' feeling, but couldn't figure out why I should be feeling this way. Driving home, I knew I needed to process this feeling or risk taking it out on my family when I got home. I might yell at my wife; she would get upset with the kids; they would kick the dog and the dog would bite the cat. The neurotic cat would wander around wondering what was going on. (We don't actually have a dog or a cat, but the part about getting angry with my wife occasionally happens.)

So I asked the Holy Spirit to show me what was going on in me. What was this 'down' feeling signalling to me? I went back in my mind from the last class to the first class, looking for clues for why I was feeling frustrated. Remembering that first class of the day, I recalled this angry student who had criticized me. Even though I had dismissed the student's anger at that time, it had registered in me and it had hurt. I had carried anger in me toward this student for his outspoken criticism. Being somewhat insecure about my teaching ability, I worried that his criticism of me was justified. I was angry with myself for my insecurity, as well as this student, but I wasn't consciously aware of it.

After mentally processing this scenario, I realized the student had a reason for his anger. I felt the Holy Spirit directing me to learn why this student was frustrated with me and with my psychology course. When he next attended class, I asked to speak with him after the lecture. I told him that his comments after our previous class had made me realize that something was wrong. I asked him to come to my office to talk about it. Later, when he related his story to me, I understood his insecurity about my psychology course. His father was a police officer, as his grandfather had been before him. His father held great expectations for his son to follow the family tradition. Looking at his marks, I saw that he had failed the first two of six tests I gave in the course. His anxiety about failing the course turned into anger toward me. When I shared some basic study skills, and got him some help with reading comprehension, he excelled in the rest of the course. Eventually, he left criminal justice and went into social work, for which he was much more suited.

Just imagine if I had ignored this anger signal as I drove home that day. Not only would I have frustrated my wife, but I would have missed a God-given opportunity to turn my anger into something productive for this student.

Step 2 in turning anger into a 'friend' is thinking back through the causes of our anger. We must learn to process the signal that the 'anger button' gives us.

Chapter 10

Understanding What Sets Off the 'Anger Button'

Step 3: Get control of your anger

Step 3 in turning anger into a 'friend' is learning to control anger. I don't mean that we should use anger to control other people. Nor do I mean we should confuse controlling anger with repressing or burying anger. We don't use anger to manipulate others to submit to our way. We don't use anger to control other people when we feel insecure or out of control. We want to control anger because uncontrolled anger is dangerous. Buried anger is uncontrolled anger. Buried anger inevitably will control us when it slips out of that 'big black cauldron' unexpectedly. We must be in control of anger 'energy' so that it will be used for good, not evil. That is why dealing with accumulated anger from our past has great importance. Then current causes of anger can be resolved objectively without interference from buried anger.

The 'anger button' always goes off for a reason. That means there will always be a trigger that lies behind the 'anger button'. What set off the 'anger button'? Knowing what causes your anger response can help immensely in gaining control of the energy that anger generates in you. Here are some potential triggers for anger. Can you identify with any of them?

Disappointment

Have you just experienced some disappointment? Perhaps you have struggled with unmet expectations. Or it could be a disappointment you have been wrestling with for years. When you carry expectations from others and those expectations are not met, you will struggle with disappointment. Disappointment can lead easily to low-level anger that you fail to recognize as anger. When your expectations from a relationship are not forthcoming, you experience disappointment, which triggers anger in yourself.

Ridicule

Have you been through a period of time in which you have been ridiculed for what you said or did? Ridicule demeans us because it minimizes our significance. Nobody enjoys ridicule. We feel hurt when people treat us this way. This hurt will automatically produce anger in you. Because ridicule is dangerous to your self-esteem, it triggers your 'anger button' immediately. I have watched how children respond to ridicule, my own included. When one child ridicules another, there is an automatic reaction of hurt and anger in the other child.

Betrayal

Betrayal ranks as one of the most difficult hurts of life. Have you ever been betrayed by a trusted friend? Betrayal is hurtful because it is usually unexpected. When you place significant trust in another person, you are caught 'off guard' if he or she betrays you. In Psalm 55 David makes reference to a close friend who betrayed him and the pain he experienced. That friend could have been Ahithophel, his confidant and counsellor. When Ahithophel went to Absalom's camp to join his rebellion, David was deeply wounded. Jesus also experienced betrayal. Betrayal may have been the most painful emotional experience in the events leading up to Jesus' death. Betrayal, especially by Judas, and by all the disciples when they deserted him in the Garden, was unimaginably painful. This is one of the reasons why divorce is so difficult. Divorce is a betrayal of the promises of covenant marriage. All betrayal produces an angry response that must be resolved through forgiveness.

Abuse

All types of abuse inflicted on you automatically produce anger. Whether the abuse occurred years ago, in your childhood, or you are currently in an abusive situation, anger is the natural response in your body to deep pain and hurt. Many people are surprised that abuse from the past continues to haunt them in the present. But time alone does not heal the serious hurt that physical, sexual or emotional abuse inflicts.

False guilt

False guilt used against you triggers an angry response. To understand false guilt, we must first understand true guilt. You must distinguish between true guilt, which is a gift from God, and false guilt, which comes from Satan, which he uses to falsely accuse you. True guilt is a signal sent by God's Spirit. It enables you to see you have stepped outside the boundaries of God's ways and protection. True guilt is your friend, not your enemy. It is designed for your protection. True guilt is meant to bring confession, which agrees with God, followed by repentance, which means changing your thinking. Repentance then changes the direction of your behaviour.

Guilt, a very powerful motivator, may drive people into insanity, if they haven't worked out their past true guilt issues. The answer for dealing with true guilt is Jesus' forgiveness, which always remains available. False guilt, on the other hand, occurs when the power of guilt is used against you in a harmful way. It is manipulation. It is motivating someone through the power of guilt. Most parents, if they are honest with themselves, will admit that they have used false guilt to motivate their children to obey. Do you know what I mean by that? For example, we might say, 'If you really love me, you will do such and such for me.' That's manipulation. Rather, we need to say to our children in a straightforward manner, 'I would like you to do this for me, please.' Never coerce them by using false guilt. As parents, we have authority from God to direct our children's lives. We want our children to obey us because obedience is right, not because we threaten them with the removal of our love when they don't obey. When false guilt is used to motivate you, anger arises because you are aware you are being manipulated. False guilt is danger to you which causes the 'anger button' automatically to go off in you.

Abandonment

Abandonment is another painful experience that will trigger anger. In numerous childhood experiences, people have been physically or emotionally abandoned by their parents, leaving them with deep scars of pain, and along with that pain, buried anger. This abandonment could come from a father whose preoccupation with his career left little time for his children. Unfortunately, many of these children live with this sense of abandonment for the rest of their lives. Or perhaps a mother who was unable to give of herself emotionally caused her children to struggle for survival on their own. Emotional abandonment creates anger in children even if they are not immediately aware of it. Adoption is another abandonment issue. It is well known that adopted children have to eventually work through their anger caused by their abandonment at birth (or later in life), even when they are adopted into secure, loving homes.

Rejection

For everyone, the most hurtful experience in life is rejection. Because our greatest need in life is unconditional love, rejection is tremendously painful. If unconditional acceptance is a universal desire, as many believe, then clearly, we don't want rejection. When someone rejects us, we experience significant hurt. This hurt automatically produces anger in us. If not resolved, this anger becomes bitterness. When people experience rejection in childhood, as adults they are afraid to receive love. They build walls to protect themselves from the hurt of rejection. Yet these walls are the very things that prevent them from experiencing the love they so badly want. Living their lives with caution, they experience the ongoing pain of rejection. That is why they are so often full of anger toward life and other people. The solution to this rejection dilemma is to receive God's unconditional love and forgiveness, through which we are healed and restored in our relationships.

Humiliation

Another hurt that causes our 'anger button' to go off is humiliation. Whether someone sets out to purposely humiliate you or does it unconsciously, being exposed and 'put down' is painful. Nobody enjoys being humiliated. Almost everyone has experienced humiliation at some point. You can feel the anger rising when someone has been taunting and teasing you about a sensitive issue. Hurt, which goes deep into your soul, releases anger automatically to defend your honour and reputation.

Deception

Deception is another stimulus that arouses anger. Whether we are deliberately deceived by someone, particularly someone we trust, or we are inadvertently let down, the 'anger button' will sound its alarm. We do not like having our trust violated. It makes us feel very vulnerable. Distrust in a friend creates anger in us. This anger is designed to protect us from continuing deception. Unless deception is confronted and resolved, the friendship will suffer damage, even irreparable damage. If anger is to be of use, it must be directed toward confronting the person who has deceived us, rather than used to build larger walls.

Intimidation

Intimidation can also trigger the 'anger button'. Whenever a person tries to force us to do what we don't want by 'blackmailing' us, anger rises in our bodies. We resent pressure from others that pushes us to do what we do not want to do. When someone uses power to force us into submission, anger arises at the injustice of the situation. If the person is too powerful to confront, we may do what he asks, but we will be angry both at him and at ourselves for submitting to the pressure.

The more we understand issues that cause our anger, the better we are able to use anger for its intended purpose – for our defence. By understanding what triggers the 'anger button', we can re-examine the incident and overcome the hurt that causes the anger. Our goal is to use the anger energy to combat the danger facing us. However, when life's hurts accumulate through time, discerning the causes of anger becomes difficult. We must first start with conscious memories of past hurts. It is there that we begin our forgiveness process. Then we can better deal with current areas of hurt, working those through to healing. Over-reaction to something in the present indicates roots of unresolved hurt in our more distant past. Over-reaction to someone's hurting words in the present serves as a clue to deeper, unhealed pain from our past that needs resolving.

Chapter 11

Anger Can Help Us Change

Step 4: Use anger's power to motivate

Once we understand why the 'anger button' signalled us, we can explore how to use that anger productively. Many people try to use anger to change the person who hurt them rather than change their own circumstances. However, that approach has a problem; we cannot change others, we can only change ourselves. So the question we need to ask is: how can I change my attitude toward my circumstances?

One of the cardinal rules of counselling that I follow is that you cannot change anyone else. You can only change yourself. In counselling, when a person shares their pain and hurt, I say to them, 'I want you to be really clear on one principle: you cannot change people who have hurt you so badly. You can only change yourself! What are you willing to work on?' The counselling process promotes changes in you that eventually effect changes in others. Thus, if you seek counselling, prepare to make changes in yourself. Do not try to change the person who has hurt you.

However, the first step in counselling is for the counsellee to know that he has been heard and understood in the hurt and pain he has suffered. Anger must be legitimized and acknowledged so that it can be worked through to forgiveness. Then, the remaining anger energy must be turned into a motivation for change in the counsellee. To move in a helpful direction, you must first address the bitterness stored in your soul. Then, using the remaining anger energy, you are motivated to make changes in your own life. This will not be done solely by your own effort. You will need the Holy Spirit to assist you in making changes. Your role is to cooperate with the Holy Spirit. His work is showing you truth and empowering you to change your heart, mind and attitude.

Change yourself

To overcome life's hurts, you must learn to change your reactions to the hurts people inflict upon you. If you want to stay in charge of your life, not allowing others to control you, you cannot succumb to reacting through negative emotions. How can you respond positively to the person or circumstances that hurt you? To avoid being repeatedly victimized, you must make changes within yourself. Remember, you cannot change another person. The best way to begin is to clean out any bitterness from the past (the 'big black cauldron'). Then you are better prepared to handle present issues of anger that occur daily. In counselling, the 'presenting' issue often is not the 'real' issue. We react as we do to certain people, seeing them as irritating, because there are unresolved past issues that cause our reaction to them.

We must learn to use anger's power as motivation in overcoming our 'victim mentality'. When we view ourselves as wounded and hurt, we transmit unconscious signals that people can get away with hurting us. Victims feel powerless to help themselves. But that is just the point. They are not powerless, because all victims have the power of anger inside. It is true that the stored anger should be worked out, but at the same time a measure of this anger needs to be retained to use as power to confront those who continually hurt us. Instead of using anger energy to retaliate or take revenge, we should use the anger energy to examine what needs to be changed in ourselves. Anger used in a negative way is wasted. Instead of anger destroying relationships, our immune system, our emotional systems or our marriage, anger should be used for good. The power of anger can be used to help us move out of our 'victim mentality', away from our fears, out of revenge thinking and into a constructive process of change. In any relationship, change in one person inevitably leads to change in the relationship. You cannot change another person directly, but you can change the relationship by changing yourself. If you change yourself, you will no longer relate to another person in the same way.

Chapter 12
Anger and Shame

Step 5: Deal with the shame of anger

In our culture, and in other cultures I have observed, there is an unwritten rule which says expressing anger is 'bad'. Even 'feeling' angry is perceived as 'bad'. The result is that we feel ashamed when we express any anger. Shame makes us want to hide whatever we feel ashamed of. Shame prevents us from dealing with or talking about anger issues. The shame of anger is similar to the shame associated with alcoholism. In order to overcome alcoholism one must break the shame barrier associated with it.

Experiencing shame is like walking down the main street in your underwear. Something just doesn't feel right. It is like one of those dreams that we occasionally have where we are doing something in the dream, but we lack control over the circumstances. We feel shame in the dream but are dragged along by the flow of the nightmare. We feel that something isn't right in the dream, but we can't get things to change. We are not in control of our dream. Often, we feel the same about our anger. It controls us. We feel shame that we cannot control it.

Two types of shame

There are two types of shame: positive and negative.

Positive shame concerns boundaries. Like breathing air, it is necessary for life. For example, we wear clothes to cover our bodies, because we have a built-in sense of positive shame. We are aware that running around naked is not acceptable. A healthy society needs positive shame, or it becomes a shameless society that eventually will implode. Negative shame, on the other hand, concerns hiding. Negative shame acts like a 'locked door'. What lies behind this locked door we don't want anyone to know. Sometimes, we won't even allow our own minds to think about what's behind that door. Often, people in counselling have hidden issues behind the issues they present to the counsellor. They won't allow the counsellor to touch those inner issues, because they don't yet trust him or her. The power of shame keeps the door of their hearts locked. They don't know as yet whether the counsellor can be trusted to handle their shame issues with sensitivity, compassion and wisdom. Eventually, when they develop trust, they offer key information that unlocks the 'shame door'. Then the counsellor can proceed with exploration that releases further healing.

Behind our 'shame doors' lies a great deal of unresolved anger. You know it is wrong to maintain bitterness toward a person, but you don't want to release it because you were hurt so badly. Or, you feel ashamed of your handling of your anger expression, and you are aware that you need to respond to issues better. Or, you cannot handle discussing anger openly because of your family background – in your family, discussing anger was considered shameful and taboo. Although anger was expressed destructively all the time, the subject was never discussed. Still today, you find it difficult to talk about your anger or your feelings of anger accumulating inside. Shame makes it difficult for you to work on your issues of anger.

Silent vows

When you express anger in a manner you deem unacceptable, you vow never to express anger like that again. I call this a silent vow because it is usually made quite unconsciously. However, a day or two later, when anger spills over again, you find you have broken your vow not to use anger in a wrong way. Of course, you feel ashamed of breaking your vow so quickly. So you make another vow to work on your anger, only to repeat the cycle again. Thus, the 'shame door' becomes further 'padlocked'. Now it is even more difficult to deal with the anger behind the 'shame door'. Because you are unable to resolve the anger issues, anger is increasingly repressed, yet the shame prevents you from being aware of it.

Let me suggest something. We need to shift our thinking. Feeling anger is normal; not feeling anger is abnormal. Because feeling anger seems abnormal, we unconsciously repress anger feelings. We deny we are feeling angry toward another person. We think there is something wrong with us when we have angry feelings toward others. Angry feelings are not wrong. Rather, it is how we express anger that is often wrong. God gave us anger for protection from danger. When the 'anger button' goes off, we are alerted to danger. We need to use our awareness of anger to trace the cause of our anger.

Using anger constructively

What we do with anger when it arises is a choice we make. Anger can be used constructively for dealing with the danger that is confronting us. Or, it can be used destructively to 'tear someone's face off', making that person pay for hurting us. Anger is given to us by God to motivate us to confront a person courageously in dealing with what he or she did to hurt us. Of course, we cannot properly confront our offender until we have worked through our issues with him or her. Otherwise, we will continue to bury our anger, locking it behind the 'shame door'. Because feelings of anger take us to the source of our pain, we can use them for our healing. This is the process we must go through to heal life's hurts. We must discover the source of our pain to begin the journey.

However, sometimes the pain is so devastating that it seems cruel to ask someone to relive it in order to open it up again for healing. Medical doctors face the same dilemma when they tell a patient that he or she needs an operation. 'The surgery will be painful,' they explain. 'The recovery will require convalescence, and you will need to adjust your schedule. The alternative to this painful operation is possible death. So what would you like to do?' Although neither option is appealing, anyone in his right mind will choose surgery rather than a funeral.

In the counselling process, I sometimes present the above scenario to my clients. I say, 'I know there will be pain in delving into your hurting past, but the alternative is to live in increasing pain as the hurt accumulates. Do you want to continue living in survival mode, or do you want to complete the operation? Do you want healing that could change the direction of your life?'

My own pastor presented this scenario to me many years ago. I am thankful that I chose the 'surgery' rather than mere survival. I have seen many other people's lives changed as a result of choosing healing. It was hard, costly and painful, but well worth the price to see the amazing changes that God brings.

To the degree we expressed anger destructively in our past or present, feeling ashamed is appropriate. Shame, as one of our emotions, signals us that we are covering things up that need to be worked out. If positive shame causes us to re-evaluate our strategy for processing anger, then it has served us well. It is much better to face our shame and work through issues than to continue living in the hidden place of shame.

Unlocking the door of shame

My three older children have paid me numerous compliments in their greeting cards and verbal expressions through the years. What they have appreciated most is my openness as a father to deal with how I have wronged them. I am not bragging about my fathering ability. I have been humbled many times by the mistakes I have made with my children. But it is much better for a father to own his wrongs than to hide them, for fear that his children will reject him. Hiding the wrongs behind the 'closed door' of shame only brings more rejection. Parents who deal honestly with their children in hurting relationships gain more respect from their children, not less. I have been inconsistent as a father in training my children, but at least I have tried to be consistent with them in owning my wrongs. Many parents, living in the shame of hidden anger from the past, try various ways of making amends with their children. The best resolution comes from humbling yourself, then seeking forgiveness for anger used destructively.

If anger is locked behind the 'closed door' of shame, we cannot change the way we deal with it. Our capacity to experience anger provides a basis for learning to use anger correctly. If we can't make changes in our behaviours, then we are doomed to continually repeat the cycles of destructive anger. These cycles are often generational. Grandfather passed them to father who, in turn, passed them to his son. Perhaps it was grandmother who passed the cycle to mother, who then passed it to her daughter. Or it can cross the gender lines and father can pass it on to his daughter as well as to his son. This cycle of destructive use of anger will continue unless someone in the family system agrees to halt it within himself. Perhaps you are the one in your family willing to deal with buried anger. You can't change your parents or grandparents but you can change yourself. If you deal with your own baggage, there is always the possibility that it could impact other family members.

To sum up this topic of shame and anger, let's make this statement: Feeling ashamed of anger is inappropriate, because God gave us anger for a constructive purpose. However, when we express anger destructively we do need to acknowledge the shame we feel. Then we ask ourselves if we should correct the way in which we have expressed anger. If shame motivates us to seek help with our anger and change the destructive ways in which we express it, then in that sense shame becomes beneficial.

Chapter 13

Developing a Strategy to Deal with Anger

Let's now move from this discussion into a practical plan for properly expressing anger. We need a strategy for acting responsibly when anger forms in us. To illustrate this process, I will share a story about my family in which anger needs to be worked through. This scenario did not happen to us as I have detailed here, but realistically, it could have happened.

Let's say that our son Andy is sixteen years old. Having obtained his driver's licence a few weeks ago, he is slowly developing confidence in his driving ability. One Friday evening he asks me for our car to visit some friends. All you parents are aware of the thoughts that go through your minds when that request comes. You want to trust your son or daughter; but, nevertheless, you feel apprehensive because of their inexperience. So, I tell Andy he may use our car on the condition that he return home by midnight.

'Are we in agreement?' I ask.

'Yes,' says Andy, 'I agree to be home by midnight.'

As he leaves home, I pray protection over him and our vehicle. About 11:30 p.m., my wife Sherry and I are planning to retire but decide to wait up a few more minutes to hear about Andy's evening. Twelve o'clock comes and Andy is still out. 'Oh,' I think to myself, 'he's probably going to be a few minutes late.' But I am perturbed that he hasn't arrived home by the stipulated time. (This is the first indication that anger is forming in me!) A half-hour passes and Andy is still not home. After another hour, I have not heard from him. Because I forgot to ask him where he was going, I can't contact him (obviously, this story takes place before the age of mobile phones). By now I feel great anxiety and increasing anger because of Andy's lateness. I lie down on the couch, wondering what to do next, and I drift off to sleep. At 3:00 a.m. I awake to hear our vehicle coming up the driveway.

By now, my red-hot anger is about to explode. Yet, I don't want to make a bad situation worse by saying or doing things I will regret. So how do I deal with the anger that is 'crouching at the doorstep'? Let's go back through the steps I have already given in this book.

Awareness of the 'anger button'

The first step is a realization that the 'anger button' has been triggered. In the scenario I have just presented, anger is obvious. My awareness of my anger is acute. But even when our anger is obvious, we often don't recognize how we are dealing with it. We just react to the situation before considering the best way to respond to the anger. Although we may feel the anger, we also must acknowledge to ourselves that we are angry. This is the first step in controlling the anger. Without acknowledgment, we explode through the emotion of anger rather than taking charge of it. So we acknowledge consciously, 'I am angry.' If we find we are frustrated, which is low-grade anger, we must also acknowledge that we are angry. Storing low-grade anger eventually will cause an explosion of rage. By acknowledging anger we have better control of it.

Why are we angry?

To control anger, we need a strategy for dealing with the situation we face. Step two is asking ourselves why we are angry. Realizing we may have little time, we must try quickly to assess what has made us angry. In this scenario, I realize that my anger is from hurt that my son has been insensitive to my feelings. 'He has no idea what he has put me through in the last few hours,' I think. His insensitivity is danger to me and makes the 'anger button' go off. I am also angry because I have been betrayed, which causes a high level of anger. Betrayal is difficult to forgive. My son has broken his trust with me. He said he would be home by midnight, yet he arrives at three o'clock in the morning. Thirdly, I am angry because I have been worried and anxious about his safety. Nobody likes living in a state of anxiety. Accumulated anxiety creates anger because it is danger to us. Anxiety is a form of fear. Fear signals danger to us. Whenever we sense danger, the 'anger button' goes off. When we quickly understand why we are angry, we are back in control of the anger. Rational control takes over from emotional reaction.

What are our goals?

The third step is to address what we want from the power of our anger. What are our goals? Because anger is energy, it can empower us to do good. Can I turn anger into good, instead of anger becoming destructive to me? So, what do I want from my situation? I want my son to understand the depth of my feelings and what I have just been through. Because he is not a father yet, he has no understanding of what he has put me through. I realize he will not understand the role of a father until his time comes, but I want him to understand something of what it is like to be in my shoes.

Another goal is teaching my son that breaking his promises is unacceptable. I want to trust him in the future; breaking his promise to me does not build trust. If I can't trust him, then I will not want to allow him to use the car again. So I want him to know that when he gives his word, keeping it becomes crucial for ongoing trust in our relationship. I might say, 'Next time you must either call me or somehow notify me that you are going to be late. I don't want to face this scenario again.' (Today, I would probably buy him a mobile phone!)

Thirdly, I want Andy to realize that his lateness threatens me, causing me to feel anxious. I don't like feeling worried and anxious. I don't want anxiety arising every time I give him the car keys. I also want to express to Andy that he is deeply valuable to me and that his safety is very important to me.

Getting back in control

How can I accomplish these three goals? Let's be realistic here. I know myself well enough to know that if I deal with this situation at three o'clock in the morning, it will probably get out of control. I need time to cool down to get in control of my anger. I want the process to be instructive – not just taking anger out on my son, Andy. So I might say to Andy, 'I am relieved to see you because I have been worried about you. But I am too upset to talk tonight. I will resolve this problem with you tomorrow morning at ten o'clock.' This may appear to put off the issue, but the delay is designed specifically to help me get in control. I realize that I may not sleep much that night, but it is the price I pay as a father. I know I need to release my anger to God through prayer. (A number of the psalms in the Old Testament are anger-releasing prayers. David and others learned to express their anger to God, working it out in prayer.) 'Father, I am angry at my son for what he put me through. But I know at times I have angered you by my sin, so help me release my anger toward Andy so I can use it righteously tomorrow morning.' This prayer allows me to bring my anger to a level in which I can use it, but it won't use me.

Working it out

In the morning, I want our meeting to be short and to the point. I don't want to berate him repeatedly, or I will lose this teaching opportunity. The first thing I want to do is listen to his story and his point of view. 'Please tell me what happened last night.' If I don't listen to him first, I may embarrass myself. What if a legitimate reason caused him to be late?

Suppose he says, 'Dad, on my way home last night I came across the scene of an accident. Two people were dead, with others badly injured. I was first one at the scene. I got so involved helping that I forgot the time. When the police came, I gave statements to them. When I left the party, I knew I was going to be about ten minutes late arriving home, but I wasn't expecting to get home as late as I did. That's what happened.'

Obviously, had I exploded in rage the previous night, I would now feel embarrassed. Here he is a hero, but I didn't take time for his side of the story.

On the other hand, he may tell me, 'Dad, I know you will find this hard to believe, but I had five flat tyres on the way home. That's why I was so late. Honest, Dad!'

And I would probably respond with a satirical grin, 'Sure you did, son. Millions wouldn't believe you, but I do!'

Whatever the reason is, I want to hear his perspective. He may simply say, 'Dad, I totally forgot about the time. I was having such a good time with my friends that I lost track of time. It was thoughtless of me to have put you through this worry.'

If I treat him with dignity, the chances are good that I can develop something positive in all of this. Having heard his side of the story, then I want him to hear my side. What is my agenda? What do I want from the power of my anger? What are my goals in this event? I want Andy to appreciate the depth of my feelings, to know that our agreements must be kept in the future, and to see that his lateness threatens me, leaving me fearful about his safety. I don't want to experience that anxiety again. I am establishing my expectations for the future. 'Andy, this is what I want from you when using my car the next time.'

Now, what if I have already exploded in anger toward him as he came in the door last night? How do I deal with the failure of using anger wrongly? I don't need to apologize for my anger but I do need to apologize for expressing my anger destructively. I can say: 'Andy, I am not proud of the way I treated you last night. It was wrong of me to have jumped all over you the minute you came in the door. I was angry for what you put me through, but I have no right to treat you that way. Would you please forgive me?' Then I can be free to hear his side of the story, expressing to him my concerns and future expectations.

I do want him to clearly understand that driving is a privilege, not a right. Driving is a reward for responsible behaviour. In the future he must be responsible for his time limits and for keeping his word. Building trust between us is crucial if he hopes to use my vehicle in the future. If punishment is warranted for breaking his word, then I need to administer a legitimate penalty that fits the crime.

Lowering our anger levels

The best way for us to lower our anger levels is to develop greater security in our lives. Because anger is largely caused by our perception of danger, our view of danger greatly affects the way we react to it. The more secure we are in knowing who we are, the less perceived danger we face. Alternatively, the more insecure we are, the more dangers we perceive. While great danger may not be there, if we perceive it as danger, it will be danger for us. For example, if I am afraid of the dark, I will perceive a great deal more danger in the darkness than someone who is not afraid of the dark. Our insecurity will create anxiety, which in turn will cause anger to rise in us. That is why we need to evaluate our pasts to challenge the lies that have become part of our lives. Our long-range goal, therefore, is to increase our security so that we lessen potential threats.

In order to deal effectively with dangers that we face daily, we must pursue a long-range goal of self-esteem growth and personal development. This is a life-time project. There is no magical formula for becoming a secure person. But every day we can make choices that will move us in the direction of being secure in who we are. The other option is to remain in the insecurity of our false perceptions.

Chapter 14

My Journey In and Out of Anger

Allow me, now, to share from my own journey, a journey of gradually coming from insecurity to growing freedom. I want to share with you how God worked a greater level of security in me.

I grew up in a family with six children, as I mentioned earlier. Both my parents were Christians who loved the Lord and desired to raise their family in a godly manner. In comparison to stories I have heard in counselling over the years, I grew up in a healthy, well-balanced family. This is not to say it was a perfect family – not by a long shot.

My parents both married at the age of thirty-four, just after the Second World War. My father fought in the war and was wounded in Sicily in 1943. He spent two years in hospital in England and Canada recuperating. My mother, Marjorie, a nurse for eighteen years, seemed glad to leave her career to marry her long-time friend, Ralph. In the next six years, they had six children, including two sets of twins. I was one of those twins. My brother, Grant, and I were twins, as were our sisters, Lynne and Elaine. Judy, the oldest, was a year older than Grant and me, and Ross was about three years younger than we were.

Wrestling with inferiority

Growing up in this 'reasonably' healthy family of six

children, I struggled greatly with feelings of inferiority to my twin brother, Grant. He was my best and closest friend. We did virtually everything together. The issues in our relationship were not his issues; they were mine. He didn't know how I felt toward him until years later, when I asked him if he was aware of my struggle with inferiority. He didn't know how I was feeling. He felt neither inferior, nor superior to me (as far as I know). He was just being himself.

I remember becoming aware of these feelings as I started school at five years of age. (Of course, I wasn't aware at that age that these feelings were called inferiority.) It seemed, in everything we did together, I could not compete and measure up. As much as my parents tried to avoid competition, overcoming it with twins was difficult. Others always compared us. There was competition with regard to friendships, work, school, sports and lifestyle.

In particular, I remember that sports days at school were the dread of my life. On the one hand I enjoyed them because I liked sports. But, on the other hand, I hated the inevitable outcome of sports days. In our age group, there were only three of us who raced together – a fellow named Larry, my brother Grant and me – because we were half a year younger than all the other children in our grade (our birthdays were in December). After each race we were given a ribbon to wear on our shirts. Blue was for first place, red was for second and a white ribbon was for third place. At the end of each sports day, I walked around school with a chest full of white ribbons. It felt like I was telling everyone what a loser I was. I came last in every race. Fortunately, many of the students did not know that only three of us entered each race. Grant and Larry shared the blue and red ribbons.

In school, I could not keep up with Grant either. He

remained one step ahead. He was sharper and quicker in all his schoolwork. In school sports, like soccer, I was placed in the back on defence while he was placed in front as a goal scorer. In baseball, he played infield while I played outfield, where I could cause less damage. In friendships, I was aware that others preferred him over me. I was sensitive by nature and cried more easily. He seemed to take things in his stride and wasn't bothered as much by friends' unkind comments.

Trying to be 'somebody'

As I grew up with inferiority and insecurity, I tried to be 'somebody'. I lived in the lie that I was inferior to just about everyone. In my teenage years, I remember thinking that if I could out-perform my brother in one thing, I could prove to myself that I was not inferior to him. (Of course that is another lie in itself.) I chose football to prove it. I remember being aggressive, getting into fights because I was trying to prove my toughness. Fighting was my way of dealing with my inferiority. Perhaps I was never better than Grant (I probably wasn't!), but I thought I was. I was using the principle of compensation. I compensated for my weaknesses by concentrating on my strengths. Although I was using the wrong motive, it helped me escape from feelings of inferiority temporarily.

After working for a year after leaving school, I entered theological college. In four years at college, I discovered that I had more academic ability than I had ever dreamed of. I also realized that I have an analytical mind. I understood behaviours (some, anyway) and analysed various causes. Unfortunately, this skill also manifested itself in my becoming critical of others. I could see shortcomings in other people but, in my inferiority, I used this to bolster my sagging self-esteem. Eventually, I was amazed to discover that I had strong intellectual ability – something which had completely escaped my attention in high school. (I'm sure it had escaped my teachers' attention too!)

So I came to this conclusion: 'This is how to overcome my feelings of inferiority. I'll stay in education for years.' I realized in later years that this was not my only motive for pursuing university training. But I do believe God was working to direct my life, despite my mixed-up motives for pursuing this career direction. However, my hidden motive said, 'I must prove that I'm smart.' So, as life went on, I began to catch glimpses of a drive in me that created problems for people around me. It produced problems for my wife, Sherry, and for my children and friends, because I needed to win at everything. I hated losing at anything, because it confirmed what I felt deep inside me: 'I'm inferior.' One way of dealing with this sense of inferiority was to take control wherever possible.

Managing anger through control

As a result, I became a controlled and controlling person (although I would have denied it at the time). I planned every event to avoid failure. I was careful to avoid situations that were too difficult to handle. This strategy worked relatively well (from my point of view) until I married. Through the first two years of marriage, I was very much in control. Sherry didn't challenge me much and left me in charge. Gradually I realized how dreadfully shallow and wrong this was for our marriage.

After fifteen months of marriage, we had our first child, Sam. The baby added another complication to my need to be in control. Babies do not necessarily fit into the well-laid plans of adults, and Sam was no exception. I was pursuing graduate studies at university. Sam was a baby 'blessed' with colic in his early months. He slept only two hours at a time. I remember being so frustrated with Sam because I couldn't control him and his screaming. I lost control and didn't know how to handle it.

As time went on, the family grew. Sarah was born two years later, with Andy arriving sixteen months afterward. Fortunately both were easy babies, but my control issues remained. As Sam grew older, I realized that facets of his personality agitated me. I would react in anger at some of his behaviours, feeling terribly guilty for how I treated him. Sometimes it was like a mirror. I saw aspects of myself that I didn't like in my son. Because I knew that the way I expressed my anger was wrong, I would store it, denying that I was angry. (I called it patience!) Then, when the repressed anger exploded, I vowed I wouldn't do that again. But the process repeated itself many times. I saw in this pattern of my behaviour a reflection of how my father treated his children. He too was generally a patient man. But some of that patience, I now believe, was buried anger. (Since my father died before Andy was born, I never explored this pattern with him.)

Generational patterns of anger

Isn't it interesting how generations repeat patterns of behaviours? I have vivid memories of certain events in the Bretherick family in which I grew up. We lived in a big, old house in south Vancouver, British Columbia. My parents, six children and grandparents all lived in this large house. (My grandparents lived in a suite in the basement of our home for fifteen years.) For many years, my brothers and I slept in the same upstairs bedroom. My twin brother, Grant, and I shared a double bed. Unfortunately, our bedroom was situated right above our parents' bedroom. Now that's a recipe for disaster! Because my father arose early in the morning for work, he was unimpressed when his boys were noisy at night rather than going to sleep.

When we were particularly noisy after he was in bed already, he would stand at the bottom of the stairs calling out, 'Boys, it's time to be quiet; please go to sleep. I don't want to hear any more noise from you.' We would try our best to settle down. But you can imagine the problem for two brothers, seven, eight or nine years old, in the same bed trying to obey that command to be quiet. When my foot slipped to Grant's side of the bed, the war would be on again. So, my father would come to the foot of the stairs, calling louder this time, 'Boys, I want you to go to sleep. No more fooling around.'

We tried our best to go to sleep because we knew what would happen if we didn't. After a quiet period of ten or fifteen minutes, we would start once more. Again, my father would come to the foot of the stairs, and this time he would say in a stern voice, 'This is your last warning!' By the fourth occurrence, there were no more warnings. At this point, my father's patience had run out. He bounded up the stairs two at a time. As soon as we heard the creak of the stairs, we knew what was about to happen. My father would come after us in his anger. Although he didn't hurt us in any significant way, we were very frightened. Sometimes my poor mother would be at the bottom of the stairs pleading with my father to 'go easy' on us.

Patience or buried anger?

Please understand that I love and respect my father very much. He was a good and godly man. He died in 1978, just before I turned thirty. I wish, to this day, he had lived for many more of my adult years. But I share this story because it is part of the reality of my growing-up years. When I was fifteen or sixteen years old, I remember vowing, 'When I grow up and have a family, I will never treat my children the way my father treated me when he was angry.' I clearly remember making that vow. However, I never resolved my anger toward my father for his treatment of me when he lost his temper. Like most people, I didn't know how to deal with my buried anger. I loved my father and thought that time would heal the hurtful aspects of our relationship.

Years later, in raising my own family, I found myself with the same issues with our oldest son, Sam. Like my father, I would be patient until I lost my temper. Then Sam received the results of my explosive anger. I vowed not to do this again, but a few days or weeks later, the anger would explode again. I was filled with guilt and shame over my uncontrollable anger. Here I was, a psychologist and pastor, helping many others, but not able to help myself.

When Sam was nine or ten years old, I exploded again over something he did or said. I hit him with the back of my hand, knocking him down. He fell, hitting his head on a counter-top, cutting himself. I stood there and wept over my uncontrollable anger. Feeling at a loss, I knew I needed help, but at that time I didn't know where to go for counsel. In my shame, I cried out to God, 'Help me, God! I need to know what is happening inside that makes me explode like this.' At that moment, the Holy Spirit brought to my memory the times when my father treated me this way.

Connecting with the past

By this time my father had been dead for seven or eight years. I obviously had no present anger issues with him. I loved him and was loyal to him. Overall, he had been a wonderful father. The Holy Spirit said to me, 'You're angry at your father and you have never resolved your anger toward him.' I argued that I wasn't angry with him. He wasn't even alive for me to be angry at. The Holy Spirit said, 'You are angry with your father from your past and it is still affecting you today.' This was a new revelation to me. (This event I am telling you about occurred several years before I began my journey into the Scriptures to study the biblical concept of anger.) But I knew, instantly, in my spirit that the Holy Spirit was right. For the first time in my life, I acknowledged my anger toward my father for how he treated me when he was out of control. In prayer, I told God about my anger toward my father. I did not deny my anger any longer. I also repented of the vow I had made as a teenager that I would never treat my children the way my father treated me.

Some years later, through my friend and pastor, Duane Harder, I received healing from my feelings of inferiority. I was released from strongholds of insecurity and inferiority. Over the next six years my life slowly changed. At times I got discouraged, wanting to give up. There were times when I thought I would never change. After all, this process of anger that had built up in me had gone on for over thirty years. But I saw that if I was willing to move in God's direction, he would make the changes in me over time.

God redeems our pasts

Interestingly, a great deal of my help for others today

comes from the changes God made in me. It is not my education or my years of experience that enables me to touch other people's lives. It is what God has worked out of me and into me that represents the reality of change. To anyone asking me about a career in counselling, I say, 'Make sure you allow God to start an inner work in you before you start facilitating an inner work in others.' Obviously there are always more things that need to be worked on. We all need to allow God to do a continual inner work of transformation in our hearts.

As I said earlier, the more secure we are as people, the less we will react to perceived danger. In my life, for so many years, I perceived danger where there was no real danger. Because of my insecurity, I reacted as if there was danger. I have repented of my failures as a parent to my son, Sam. I have acknowledged my wrong, asking him to forgive me. He has, in turn, listened to me lecture in my workshops (and he has even heard me share his story – with his permission, of course). He has worked through forgiveness toward me with a friend of mine.

Even so, I know I passed some anger patterns and insecurity to him (it is inevitable). In my imperfection as a parent, I passed on to Sam a certain amount of hurt and pain. He must work through his issues, just as I have worked out mine. Because I received forgiveness both from God and from him, I do not live in guilt or shame for my mistakes. I choose not to live in regret, but to look forward to God's redeeming work in my life and in others' lives. Thank God that he is able to redeem our pasts. In working out my past, I am able to help others work out their pasts. We can only pass on to others what we are. That's why we are never finished with the process of transformation. When interactions with my wife or children surface painful realities in me, I work them out, too. I do not bury my head in the sand, pretending my failures are not real. The more I work out my issues, the more I can help others deal with their failures.

How was anger handled in your family?

Because your present anger is affected by how you dealt with past anger, it is important for you to examine how anger was handled in your family of origin. Appendix 2 is an exercise entitled, 'How Was Anger Handled in Your Family?' The exercise will help you see the correlation between your treatment as a child and your present issues as an adult. How anger was managed in your family as you grew up generally corresponds to how you handle anger today. If you don't deal with past issues of anger, working only on current anger issues, you will deal superficially with your anger. Our motive isn't blaming our parents, our families or ourselves for past hurts. Our goal is being honest about mistakes that have occurred in our families so that they can be healed. We want to do this healing without dishonouring our parents. The exercise is designed to expose any bitterness that may have accumulated from our pasts.

There are three things that this exercise is designed to accomplish:

- to help you rethink the model of anger management you have been given by your upbringing;
- to motivate you to work out bitterness that has accumulated in you;
- to reveal that everyone has issues of anger to be resolved.

Part 3

The Power of Forgiveness

Chapter 15

Distinguishing Between Anger and Bitterness

In Part 1, we defined anger and revealed how buried anger accumulates. In Part 2, we presented the skills that are necessary for managing the pressures of life that create anger responses. Now, in Part 3, we will explore the power of forgiveness – how forgiveness releases stored anger so we can be set free from the consequences of bitterness.

In my discussion about anger, I have been making a distinction between anger stored in us from accumulated past hurts (bitterness) and anger that is present in us as useful energy. This second type of anger is used productively for dangers we face every day. However, I want to make sure that the difference between anger and bitterness is perfectly clear to you. Understanding the difference between the two is crucial for using anger in the way God intended when he made you.

Anger is automatic, bitterness is a choice

Anger is an automatic, natural, God-given response in our bodies to the presence of danger. Whenever real or potential danger is present, or we perceive danger as present, the 'anger button' goes off, signalling this danger. Anger is a natural, physiological response to danger that God has built into us. If anger is used improperly, or ignored and repressed, it turns into bitterness. Bitterness, then, is a choice we make to hold the power of anger as a means of revenge. In our minds we argue, 'Because you hurt me, I am going to hurt you in return.' Bitterness is both unfulfilled revenge and unresolved anger. The *Houghton Mifflin Canadian Dictionary* defines bitterness as 'marked by anguished resentfulness'.

Once I counselled a husband and wife who were very angry at each other. The wife came in for counselling first. She was frustrated with her husband's treatment of her. He constantly expressed his bitterness in the home. He would never forgive her if she made a mistake. He berated her repeatedly and seldom praised her. She felt unable to please him. After listening to her story, I asked if she thought her husband would see me. She said, 'He'll never come; he doesn't like counsellors and psychologists.' But I encouraged her to ask anyway, and so she did. Surprisingly, he was glad to come. Perhaps he wanted to ensure that his side of the story was being heard.

Naturally, he began by sharing his grievances about her. His major complaint: his wife was more loyal to her parents, particularly her father, than to him. Over nineteen years of marriage, the loyalty issue had increasingly become a major rift, at least from his point of view. He was angry at how his wife responded much more quickly and graciously to her father than to him. This issue, along with others, turned into a deep bitterness in the husband. He was angry with both his wife's parents and his wife. I pointed out that forgiving his wife and her parents would change the relationship. But he had lived with bitterness for so long, he felt it was his right to retain his anger. He couldn't stop being angry because it was his only means of preventing his wife's family from taking advantage of him.

I couldn't seem to communicate how desperately he

needed to release his bitterness. One day, after seeing him for several counselling sessions, I decided to experiment with him. (I should never have done this, but I was getting desperate and didn't check with the Holy Spirit for direction.) I provoked him to anger to show him how he continually attacked his wife in anger. I played the 'devil's advocate' (more literally than I realized). Sure enough, he responded with anger toward me. I then said to him, 'That's exactly what you do to your wife all the time.' He looked at me with a glare, put his hat on and walked toward the door. Again I baited him by saying, 'Is that how you will spend the rest of your life – running away from your issues?' He thought for a few seconds, and his pride brought him back to his seat. I continued to pressure him to deal with his buried anger. By this time, he had had enough; again, putting on his hat, he walked toward the door. As he left, he used some rather strong language to describe his feelings toward me.

Later in the evening, I was putting my two young sons, Nathan and Caleb, to bed. In the darkness, as I was lying on the bed with Nathan, the Holy Spirit brought to my memory the incident with this man. He said to me, 'What you did to this man was wrong; I want you to rectify it.'

Naturally, I responded with delight (are you kidding? – I spent several minutes arguing with God). I finally said, 'Okay, God, what do you want me to do?' The Holy Spirit told me to call him and apologize for my behaviour. I was not eager to do it but neither was I eager to disobey the Holy Spirit.

So I phoned and said, 'John, this is Graham calling.'

There was an immediate blast of anger on the other end of the phone. He was still very upset with me for my treatment of him that afternoon.

I said to him, 'John, I am phoning to apologize for what

I said and did to you this afternoon.'

He quickly agreed how wrong my treatment of him had been. Again he released a tirade in my direction.

I spoke once more and said, 'John, I am not phoning to justify my behaviour. I am phoning to apologize and ask for your forgiveness. What I did to you was wrong and I am asking you to forgive me.'

There was dead silence for a moment and then he said, rather gruffly, 'Yes, I will.'

I said, 'Thank you, John,' and hung up.

I thought to myself, 'Well, that's the end of that, and I will never see John again, but at least my apology was right.'

About a month or two later, John's wife came to the counselling centre to pay their outstanding bill. I happened to be at the reception desk when she came in. I asked her how things were in the marriage. I wasn't expecting a positive answer. She said, 'You know, it's funny, but things have actually got a lot better since that incident between you and John.' Surprised, I asked her what happened. She said, 'Were you aware that you were the fifth person he had seen for help?' Apparently he had seen three Catholic priests, one other counsellor and me. In each counselling situation he took a hard-nosed approach of revenge toward his wife. He always asserted that he had the right to his bitterness, resulting in an argument with the counsellor. In every case, he left the counselling sessions feeling justified in retaining his anger. She said to me, 'Graham, when you phoned to acknowledge your wrong, it confused him. When you demonstrated forgiveness to him on the phone, he saw the power of forgiveness.' Very interesting! My mistake and failure, yet my obedience to the Holy Spirit, did more good than all my counselling with him. The power of forgiveness demonstrated!

Bitterness is a choice. I could have become bitter toward John for his stubbornness toward me. It would have been easy to blame him, saying I did my best. Because the Holy Spirit alerted me to my wrong behaviour and my responsibility for it, I chose obedience. God worked good through my willingness to seek forgiveness. Anger is not the problem – the stored anger in us (which is bitterness) is the problem.

Anger signals danger – bitterness is dangerous

A second difference exists between anger and bitterness. Anger is given by God to alert us to danger; bitterness is just plain dangerous. Remember, anger is not primarily an emotion; anger is energy. But because it has emotional expression, anger can function as an emotional signal. Anger is actually a friend that energizes us to fight danger, but it can also signal us when danger comes near. Bitterness, on the other hand, causes grave danger to us. All bitterness is destructive. With bitterness we are hurt twice. When someone wrongs us and we don't resolve our anger quickly, we begin to experience consequences from the bitterness. The longer we hold on to bitterness, the more destructive it becomes. It eats into our souls (sometimes, it literally eats into our bodies) and can even become a part of our personality. When we don't deal with our bitterness, we are continually living out hurt from the past. So, instead of hurting once, we continually live the hurt of that event.

Many of my clients have argued that they have a right to maintain their anger. Justice demands payback. Yes, I agree. Justice has a place, but we should not bring about our own justice. That responsibility belongs to God and those whom God appoints in government.

Once I counselled a woman sent by her doctor. She had had cancer some years earlier and there was concern that she could relapse. She was under a lot of stress and her doctor saw that she had a great deal of unresolved anger. Jean was in her mid-fifties when she first saw me. As she shared her story, I saw why she was so bitter.

When she was twenty-one years old, she was engaged. During that year of engagement, her sister, a year younger, stole her fiancé. Jean's sister married this man and from that point on, the two sisters never spoke to each other. They lived in the same small community, attended the same small rural church, but never talked to each other. In the community, everyone knew about the lingering conflict between the two sisters. Eventually, Jean married and raised her own family, but never forgave her sister for stealing her fiancé.

When Jean shared her story with me, I counselled her that forgiveness was absolutely crucial for her physical health. We wrestled with this issue of forgiveness for several sessions. I could see that it was not easy for Jean to forgive, after living with this anger for over thirty years. I explained to her repeatedly how dangerous bitterness is. I told her bitterness had probably contributed to her cancer because bitterness weakens the immune system. Now she was in danger of a relapse. Finally, Jean agreed to begin working out her buried anger toward her sister. After several weeks of counselling and moving toward forgiveness, Jean came one day with an announcement. 'My sister's husband died yesterday.' Then she had a question for me. 'Graham,' she said, 'should I go to the funeral?' I asked if she was ready to face her sister after all these years. She agreed that she was far enough along in the healing process to risk attending the funeral.

So, a few days later she went to the funeral. Not only

that, she even approached her sister at the end of the service, giving her a hug. They cried on each other's shoulders. (Apparently, the whole church was in tears!) This was their first real contact in over thirty years. As Jean shared with me, she wept at both the joy and the regret – the joy of finally reconciling with her sister but the regret at wasting so many years of relationship because of bitterness. As we continued to develop her heart of forgiveness, Jean's sister eventually acknowledged her wrong in stealing Jean's fiancé. God graciously worked out this painful relationship. The bitterness Jean had retained probably would have cost her her life, literally, if she had not worked it out.

Anger is constructive – bitterness is destructive

Thirdly, anger is constructive but bitterness is destructive. Anger helps us to see what we need to change in ourselves. Anger energy gives us courage to face present problems or conflicts. When we sense danger in a relationship, we often find ourselves afraid to confront the issue. We don't want to get hurt again. Anger actually can provide the motivation or energy to face the challenge and deal with the conflict. Anger is a constructive process designed to energize us to confront those who hurt us. Anger, expressed properly, can help rebuild damaged relationships. It enables us to confront when we need to confront. If we sense our anger demanding revenge, then we must first work out our forgiveness. Then, the remaining energy of anger can be used to confront or face the challenge.

In contrast to anger, bitterness blocks our perception of reality and becomes destructive in our lives. When we are full of bitterness, we stop perceiving clearly. It is like trying to see in a fog. Everything becomes distorted. Years ago, I remember driving north on the Calgary–Edmonton highway, coming into a dense fog. The fog was so thick that we pulled over to the side of the highway and drove on the shoulder. One of my friends walked in front of the car so we wouldn't hit anything. It was very dangerous because we easily could have collided with something without warning. Bitterness is like that. It produces a fog so we can't see clearly. People who are full of bitterness cannot see their own faults and problems. They are too busy blaming everyone else for the wrongs in their own lives.

Jim, a man in his early forties, came for counselling. Each week Jim drove from a small town, miles away. He came for counselling because he had done poorly in university some years earlier and he was angry with the professors who had failed him. He was certain he had done everything required of him to pass his courses. In his anger toward the professors, he became increasingly moody and reclusive. As the counsellor explored Jim's story, he discovered a deep root of bitterness toward his father. He blamed all his problems on his dad. Jim felt that his father never understood or accepted him while he was growing up. His father was a rugged individual who had trouble appreciating the finer aspects of life. Jim's father had a tough exterior, seldom showing his emotions, except anger.

Jim, on the other hand, was a sensitive individual. Because of this, he was vulnerable to being hurt. Many times, Jim's father treated him unkindly and gruffly. Unfortunately, his father was unaware of the emotional pain he caused his son. As a result of this rejection, Jim rebelled and dabbled in drugs and pornography. As the counsellor worked through Jim's buried anger, he asked Jim if he could see the destruction that bitterness caused in his life. Jim never had connected his anger toward his father with his present issues. The counsellor showed him that his anger toward his professors was directly connected to anger toward his father. Because of his father's treatment of him, Jim developed anger toward anyone in authority. Because God is the ultimate authority, he was also bitter toward God. Jim's anger was rooted in his relationship with his father.

So the process of working out Jim's anger was begun. The lie that he must forever be a victim of his father's treatment of him was confronted. Clearly, Jim's father's behaviour had been wrong. But Jim's reaction to his father was equally wrong in not forgiving him. Eventually, the counsellor and Jim worked through the anger to a place where he could forgive his father for the emotional abuse (and occasional physical abuse) he had suffered. What angered Jim the most was his father's emotional distance and neglect. He longed to hear affirmation and praise from his father, but it never came. It is likely that Jim's father never heard affirmation from his father, either.

Anger is useful – bitterness is useless

Fourthly, we see that anger is useful but bitterness is useless. One time a woman (I'll call her Jane) came to see me because she was angry and troubled about the way her supervisor treated her. She worked for a large organization with many employees. She was a supervisor, overseeing twenty employees, but she also had a superior over her. It was because of this supervisor that she came for counselling. She felt she had received unfair treatment from him in her annual evaluation.

As I began investigating the issues behind her initial concern, she shared that she would occasionally go on an alcoholic binge, drinking all weekend. But because it happened irregularly, she didn't see its significance. However, she was also a binge exerciser, going to extremes in exercising. She further confided that she had problems with relationships with men. She would get emotionally committed to a man, giving herself to him sexually. Then, after getting hurt in the relationship, she would avoid involvement with men for a period of time. She was a woman of extremes, vacillating between over-involvement and abstinence. I asked her if she thought that these extremes could have resulted from deep hurt in her past life. She admitted some difficulties in the past but said no more. I was aware that something was deeply troubling her but I did not know what it was. I knew it was a 'locked door' of shame but she was unwilling to open it to me, at the moment. As I continued listening to her tell her story, exploring her past, she slowly began to share her 'dark secret'.

When Jane was nine years old, her father attempted intercourse with her but was unsuccessful in penetrating. After a few more attempts, he finally succeeded in having intercourse with her when she was twelve. This sexual abuse went on regularly until she was twenty-one years old. Even when she married a young man to escape from home, her father managed to have intercourse with her two more times. At twenty-seven she was divorced because of an immense struggle with sexual intimacy. Jane held deep anger toward men, yet was strangely drawn to them. This attitude was reflected in her conflict with her male supervisor at work. I asked if she had confronted her father, after she left home. She told me she did once. 'I told my aunt [her mother's sister] about my father's sexual involvement; she went with me to confront my father.' Before they confronted her father, Jane and her aunt went to Jane's mother. Jane's mother denied that such a thing could have ever happened. Nevertheless, Jane's mother confronted her husband with the allegations. Jane's father was incensed and accused her of trying to destroy his reputation for no good reason. Three years had passed since Jane had talked with either parent.

Imagine the volcano of bitterness and pain in Jane. I told her that considerable time and energy was required to see her released from this bitterness, but that I was willing to help get her free from being her father's victim. A few counselling sessions later, she agreed to resolve her deep anger toward her father. At first, the thought of forgiving him was totally unacceptable. But finally, she saw the uselessness of holding on to her bitterness. Using the Forgiveness Exercise (see Appendix 3), she started writing. She wrote out her pain and anger and I read her writing aloud to her. At times she wept and wept at the pain she revisited; sometimes I wept with her. Week by week, she made progress. After a year and a half of counselling, Jane had worked through her bitterness and had truly forgiven her father. We concluded the weekly appointments and Jane left, a different woman.

Six months later, I noticed Jane's name in my appointment book again. When she came in I was interested to see how Jane was doing. She was doing well, but had a dilemma that needed my help. A cousin was getting married soon and her parents were invited to the wedding. She wanted to go because she was close to this cousin. Did I think she was wise to go? We met for three sessions to work through her decision. At that point, Jane decided she was strong enough to take the risk. She decided to bring a friend for moral support. This was a major step in Jane's recovery. I was delighted to see her move ahead in her growth. As it turned out, her father didn't go to the wedding; only her mother attended the ceremony. Jane sat on the opposite side of the church from her mother and never talked with her. She saw me once more after the wedding to share how pleased she was with her new freedom. Even though Jane may never be reconciled to her father, she is no longer his victim; she is free to move ahead with her own life. (Incidentally, her attitude toward her male supervisor also improved and she began to enjoy work again. She discarded the driving pressure to prove herself at work.)

God placed anger in us to provide a means to defend ourselves. Anger's power or energy enables us to confront abusive relationships. When we live as victims, we are hurt repeatedly. Anger enables us to make choices which stop the hurt. We need not be victims forever. We can use anger energy to stop the cycle of victimization. We also must confront the lies that have rendered us a victim in the first place. Victims often are passive people. They have been taught to be passive in their relationships. Sometimes it is an aspect of their temperament and personality. Often the victim needs to develop an ability to fight the passive response within. That is what the energy of anger can do. Anger can cause a person to say, 'I don't have to be like this!' Instead of anger energy turning inward, causing low self-esteem and depression, anger can serve a useful purpose.

Bitterness, on the other hand, is a negative attitude that has one desire: revenge. This attitude says, 'I have the right to pay my offender back because of what he or she has done to me.' When hurting, angry people tell me they have that right, I agree with them. But then I tell them I don't recommend asserting their rights, because bitterness is useless. Bitterness will never satisfy their longing for peace.

All hurt produces anger in us. It is the way God

created us and formed us. Hurt is danger to us; danger automatically releases anger in us for our protection. Anger is given to us by God to deal with danger around us. When we don't use anger to solve our hurts, then anger becomes buried in us.

The three most common symptoms of bitterness are blaming, revenge and judging. If we find ourselves blaming others for our issues, or criticizing others or seeking revenge toward people who hurt us, it means we possess stored anger. Whenever I hear people blaming, whether it is the government, the church, the media, their boss, or their parents, I know they have buried anger. Blaming others indicates we have unresolved anger issues to examine. The same is true with revenge. Whether revenge is active or passive, the attempt to get back at someone reveals anger that needs to be worked out. Likewise, critical thoughts toward others or negative judgments indicate buried anger. Even though we may not share our critical thoughts with others, the fact that our minds are consumed with judgments reveals buried anger within us.

The only way to release bitterness is to connect with our anger. As we consciously work out anger through forgiveness, we release anger and are set free from the consequences of bitterness. Many people are afraid to confront their anger because they believe anger is dangerous. Anger itself is not dangerous, but stored anger or bitterness is damaging. In a healthy therapeutic setting, anger can be released without becoming destructive. Anger can also be expressed in many other settings in a constructive way. It is like working with dynamite. Used as a construction tool, dynamite is valuable. But in the hands of an amateur, it is very dangerous. Anger has the potential to be dangerous but, in itself, anger exists for our good.

Ephesians 4:30–32 says: 'do not grieve the Holy Spirit of God with whom you were sealed for the day of redemption. Get rid of all bitterness, rage and anger, brawling and slander, along with every form of malice. Be kind and compassionate to one another, forgiving each other just as in Christ, God forgave you.' If Christians do not rid themselves of bitterness, they grieve the Holy Spirit. Therefore, one way to please and honour the Holy Spirit is by dealing with accumulated anger or bitterness.

It is imperative that the distinction between bitterness and anger be understood. Hurt always releases anger in us. When the 'anger button' signals danger, we have two choices. We can turn anger into positive action to solve the problem or we can store anger. When we use anger to solve problems successfully, we develop healthy attitudes toward life, and toward other people. When we resolve problems and maintain healthy relationships, we feel positive about ourselves.

If, on the other hand, we choose to repress anger, bitterness will inevitably express itself in one of four ways. Buried anger will be expressed toward others in active aggression (rage) or passive aggression (withdrawal). Or, by remaining within us, it attacks our self-esteem (leading to depression) or our bodies (leading to psychosomatic illnesses). These all are uncontrolled expressions of buried anger. Although anger may be expressed in any of these forms, our problem or hurt remains unresolved. When resentment builds in us, we feel like a victim again. Over time, we develop negative attitudes toward life. The desire for revenge increases toward those who offended us. As the bitterness grows in us, it begins to infect our personality. If the bitterness continues, the personality can eventually be dominated by bitterness. The end result can be a personality that is destroyed through mental illness, deep depression or even suicide.

The diagram on the following page encapsulates the danger of failing to deal properly with buried anger or bitterness. Continual wrong choices can draw a person down a completely wrong path.

Many of you reading this book have gone through some very difficult and traumatic encounters in life. I don't want to offer simplistic or 'cheap' answers to your painful experiences. I don't want to minimize anyone's formidable pain. Your trauma isn't related necessarily to the degree of offence you have experienced. The impact is measured not by the magnitude of the experience but by how that experience affected you. Some people emerge from traumatic experiences without huge emotional scars. Others have different responses to similar experiences that wound them significantly. Two people may experience similar events, yet may have different responses to the trauma. To help people work out their pain, the recovery work must relate to the impact that the pain had on the individual.

The Process of Bitterness

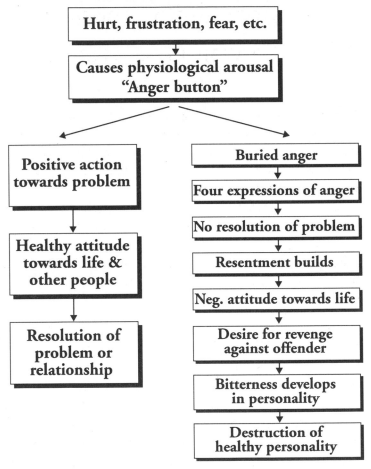

Hurt, frustration, fear, etc.

↓

Causes physiological arousal
"Anger button"

Positive action towards problem

↓

Healthy attitude towards life & other people

↓

Resolution of problem or relationship

Buried anger

↓

Four expressions of anger

↓

No resolution of problem

↓

Resentment builds

↓

Neg. attitude towards life

↓

Desire for revenge against offender

↓

Bitterness develops in personality

↓

Destruction of healthy personality

Chapter 16

Healing Bitterness Through Forgiveness

Up to this point we have focused on anger and its purpose. We have also seen the destructive nature of buried anger. Now, we want to focus our attention on the antidote to bitterness, which is forgiveness. Forgiveness is the key to overcoming buried anger.

Over my years of counselling experience, I have heard numerous reasons why forgiveness cannot solve someone's painful past. People have said to me, 'Why should I forgive? Look how much they hurt me!' Then they list the various reasons why forgiveness is totally unrealistic. These are some of their reasons.

Myth no. 1: Forgiveness is condoning

'Forgiveness condones what my offender did to me. If I forgive my offender, he can hurt me again.' From a 'victim's' point of view, I understand the concern. If we forgive, won't we be giving offenders permission to continue hurting us, and others, repeatedly? It is true that abusers can, and will, take advantage of a victim, if given that opportunity. But true forgiveness does not condone wrong and hurtful behaviour. Forgiveness does not endorse what was done to you. When Jesus hung on the cross, he said, 'Father, forgive them, for they know not what they are doing.' He wasn't saying that what they had done to him was right or that their sin didn't matter. He wasn't saying that his Father was going to 'let bygones be bygones'. A Judgment Day is coming for those who refuse to accept his offer of forgiveness. Sin is still sin. It is wrong. It is destructive. What the abuser did to you was wrong – full stop. But forgiveness is the only way you can be free from being a victim for the rest of your life.

Myth no. 2: Forgiveness is like trying to forget

People have said to me, 'I'm willing to forgive, but I will never forget what was done to me.' On the other hand, some clients have asked, 'If I have forgiven but the memory comes back, does that mean I have not truly forgiven?' There is a danger with connecting forgiving and forgetting. Often, we cannot forget traumatic events that have happened to us, even though we have truly forgiven. If we must forget in order to forgive, we may ultimately use denial to help us forgive. To deny we are angry when anger is obvious is not helpful. Anger will eventually become bitterness. By pushing it from conscious memory, we are denying the reality of what needs to be forgiven and released. However, when we forgive someone, in time that event will not be as dominant in our memories. It can still be remembered if we make a conscious effort to bring it to mind, but it will not control us any more.

Myth no. 3: Forgiveness is trying to be nice

I have met many people who confused 'being nice' with forgiveness. Clearly, these are not the same. When there are tensions in a relationship, some people opt for being nice. They try to please their offender and believe they are being biblical by 'turning the other cheek'. Being nice results in repression. We become the 'martyr' or the 'victim' in the name of trying to be spiritual. Forgiveness is not pretending to be nice. We must work through the pain, trouble or hurt that we have experienced. Although we don't want revenge on our enemies, being nice is not the same as getting in touch with our anger by purposefully releasing the offender from his offence.

Myth no. 4: Forgiveness is 'letting people off the hook'

The Bible clearly teaches that only God (and authorities that are God-ordained) is permitted to bring vengeance against another person (Romans 12:19). Anyone who hurts us is still responsible before God for the hurt they have inflicted. But it is God who holds them accountable, not us. If we make our offender accountable to us for his sin, we exercise a role that God has reserved for himself. When we let go of our right to revenge, we assign the issue to God for his righteous response of justice. If you want to ensure that you have surrendered this vengeance to God, do what Romans 12 tells you – bless your enemies. When you bless, God performs his work in the offender's life. If you use the right of revenge, God himself will turn the whole issue over to you. Trying to play God's role is a bad idea.

As I have been writing this section of the book, I am on a plane flying from India back to Canada. The in-flight movie has just finished playing – it was *Bruce Almighty*, starring Jim Carrey. In the movie, Bruce is angry with his life and thinks he can do better than God at running it. So, God pays him a visit (in the form of the actor Morgan Freeman) and gives Bruce his powers. In time, Bruce not only discovers that he doesn't do a very good job of playing God, but also causes trouble all over the world.

As I was watching the movie, I was reminded of the many times in the past when I have 'played God', taking my revenge and making things worse.

If we want the right of revenge, I believe God will give it to us. But isn't it smarter to let the God of the Universe, in his wisdom and his power, have his way with our enemies? God has an amazing way of turning life around for us. Often he turns what was done as evil toward us into something for our good. God knows when to apply the pressure and when to remove it. Romans 2:4 teaches us that the kindness of God leads men to repentance. Let's allow God to be God and do what he promises he will do to confront our enemies.

Myth no. 5: Forgiveness is magic

Forgiveness is not magical. It is hard work, takes time and often needs to be applied more than once. Quite a few years ago, I was hurt badly by a young man whom I was mentoring. Earlier I also hurt this young man, along with others in our church, by my immaturity as a leader. I unknowingly allowed a person in the church to take advantage of some other people. I was accused of protecting the wolf instead of the sheep, and there was validity to the accusation. In my ignorance and naivety, I created some damage in our church. Some people who were close, loyal friends suddenly became my 'enemies' and left the church. With the help of my pastor and mentor, Duane Harder, I was able to see my wrong and repented. I wrote to each of these people, asking for their forgiveness. But there was another side to this conflict. I, too, was hurt by their betrayal. Instead of forgiving me, they left the church.

I remember trying to work through my forgiveness

for how they hurt me. The young man I was discipling probably hurt me the most. During the summer months that followed our church split, I was painting the outside of our house. With each brushstroke, I said, 'I forgive you, Joe, I forgive you, Joe.' I don't know how many times I repeated this, but I knew I was working out my anger and turning it into forgiveness. (I was painting rather vigorously as I released my anger!) I wanted to forgive him, because I knew it was the right response, but there was a lot of anger in me. This forgiveness was hard work but well worth the effort.

A day or two after I finished painting the house, I was jogging in a park in Lethbridge. Who should be coming from the opposite direction toward me but Joe! I knew instantly that God had arranged this encounter. My first thought was, What do I do now? Then peace settled over me because I knew I had forgiven Joe and I could greet him without feeling angry or afraid. As I met him on the path, I stopped and chatted with him. He didn't know what I had just gone through but I knew the joy of forgiveness within me. As I said goodbye, I even gave him a hug. I love the power of forgiveness!

There is nothing magical about forgiveness. Forgiveness is often hard work and takes time to apply. Sometimes, we think if we have said, 'I forgive you', the forgiveness should take effect immediately. But if the pain is deep, forgiveness may need to be applied many times before its true effect is experienced. I can guarantee, however (on the basis of God's Word – Matthew 6:14–15), that if you continue applying God's forgiveness to the person who hurt you, you will experience the release and joy of forgiveness yourself.

Chapter 17
So What Is Forgiveness?

We now know what forgiveness is not. What, then, is forgiveness? I want to share three word pictures with you to convey what forgiveness is.

Forgiveness is renouncing our right to resentment

The first word picture is this: forgiveness is renouncing the 'right' of revenge. Forgiveness is renouncing resentment as a means of solving problems. When we store anger, resentment begins to build in us. We often feel we have a 'right' to our resentment because of what has been done to us. Forgiveness is deciding not to claim that 'right'. Otherwise, we become imprisoned by our 'right'. When people have argued with me, 'Don't I have the right to pay back this person?', I tell them they do have that 'right' if they want to claim it. (In truth, we have no 'right' to revenge because God, alone, claims that right.) But I assure them that if they exercise that 'right', they will be imprisoned in their resentment. However, in giving up their 'right' to resentment, and choosing forgiveness, they will enjoy a new level of freedom they have not known before.

Forgiveness is cancelling a debt

Here is a second word picture of forgiveness. Forgiveness

is like cancelling a debt. Let me tell a story to illustrate what I mean.

Let's say I have a friend named John. John and I have been good friends for many years. One day, John comes to me saying, 'Graham, I am facing a difficult situation. I need to ask you for a really big favour.'

So I say, 'Tell me what you need and I will try to give it to you.'

John says to me, 'I need to borrow $2,000 to get myself out of a scrape. I just need to borrow the money for a week and then I will be able to pay you back.'

I think to myself, 'That's a really big favour, because that's all the money I have in my savings account.'

However, I am John's loyal friend, so I agree, albeit reluctantly. (My reluctance has something to do with a vague awareness that the Scriptures say it is not wise to loan money to a friend.) So I write him a cheque for $2,000, reaffirming our agreement that he will repay it in a week. He guarantees that the loan will be repaid in full in a week.

A week goes by, and I hear nothing from John. I phone him the day after, saying, 'It's Graham calling, John.'

He immediately apologizes. 'Graham, I'm sorry, I meant to call you. I can't believe what's happening to me.' He goes on to explain his circumstances and asks me if he can please pay me back next week, instead. I say yes (reluctantly again), and we hang up.

Another week goes by, and I don't hear from John. So I phone him the next day, and as soon as he hears my voice he immediately launches into an apology, followed by the reason why he has failed to pay back the money he borrowed. This time he asks for two weeks' grace and promises to pay me back in that time. He knows he will have all his finances sorted out by then.

I say to John, 'Please make sure you do this time. I haven't told my wife I loaned you the money, and I need to get it back into our savings account.' (Not telling my wife has compounded the problem. Fear, mixed with guilt, is a powerful emotional combination and something that we can't live with for long.)

Two weeks go by and, again, I don't hear from John. So I call him the next day and, in an angry tone of voice, I remind him of his broken promise. John explains once more what he is trying to do to pay me back, and I again accept his promise to come through with the money. This scenario goes on week after week after week. Now I am consumed with anger because of this mess I am in. I can't eat very well. I am not sleeping. My stomach is upset. My job is being affected. My marriage is tense. I am well aware that I am angry with John for what he is putting me through.

So I call up a friend who is a counsellor and ask him how I can correct this situation. My counsellor friend says to me, 'As I see it, Graham, you have two choices. You can take him to court to recover your money or you could cancel the debt and forget it.'

'Cancel the debt!' I say. 'Not on your life. He owes me that money. And besides, my wife is wanting that money back in our account.'

So I go about investigating the court proceedings, only to discover that it is going to cost me about $2,000 to get my $2,000 back. Now I am even more angered. So I go back to my counsellor friend and ask him, 'What was the other alternative you suggested to me?'

He says, 'You write a note to John and tell him that you are cancelling the debt of $2,000 that he owes you.'

At this point in the saga, I am well aware that it is not worth spending $2,000 to collect the money from John. So

I write this note:

> *Dear John*
> *You no longer owe me $2,000. I am cancelling your*
> *debt. You do not have to repay the money you owe me,*
> *ever again.*
> *Yours sincerely*
> *Graham*

That's what forgiveness is. It expresses the reality that although this person owes me this debt, I am not going to collect. I am not pretending the debt isn't real. The truth is that John does owe me the money. But I am not going to claim it any more. By cancelling the debt, I am free of the burden of collecting the money. (This experience actually happened to me years ago with a close friend. It wasn't $2,000 but $500, and I never saw the money again. Once I had cancelled the debt, I was free of trying to collect it for the rest of my life. Of course, I couldn't trust this friend again in the area of finances, but I was free of my anger toward him.)

Pardoning the offender

The third word picture is the analogy of pardoning the offender. It means not demanding punishment where justice is warranted. It is like a judge who has the legal authority to sentence the guilty person, but instead chooses to pardon the convicted offender. Even though it is clear that the person has broken the law, the judge decides to apply mercy instead of judgment. Mercy is exactly what we receive from God when we ask for forgiveness for our sins. We deserve punishment – the whole weight of the law applied to our guilt. But instead we are offered pardon and mercy. That's why Jesus says we must forgive others for their offences against us, because we have been pardoned from our offences. As we were shown mercy by God, we must extend mercy to our fellow human beings. In fact, according to Matthew 18, the clearest indication that we have received God's forgiveness is that we extend forgiveness to others. The people who offended me and hurt me don't deserve mercy any more than I do. When I stand before the Eternal Judge, he says, 'Graham, you are guilty as charged [by Satan, our accuser], but I am pardoning you because your debt has been paid by my Son's death on the cross.' Amazingly, I am free from paying for it myself (which is impossible anyway).

Matthew 7:1–2 says: 'Do not judge, or you too will be judged. For in the same way you judge others, you will be judged, and with the measure you use, it will be measured to you.' Some years ago I realized that if I hold unforgiveness in my mind and heart, and even if nobody knows it, unforgiveness still has implications in my life. Jesus never told us to suspend all judgments toward others. He simply said, the same attitude with which we judge others will extend to us. If we judge others fairly, we will be judged fairly. But if we have unforgiveness in our hearts, we inevitably will judge others wrongly. What is hidden in our hearts will eventually come to the surface.

The same could be said for fear. We may try to bury (repress) our fears to avoid dealing with them, but they too eventually will surface in our behaviour. I have worked with parents who tried to hide their fears from their children, yet wondered how their children picked up these hidden fears, nevertheless. Likewise, our hidden judgments will emerge in both our behaviour and our children's behaviour. Children learn significantly about life through modelling and observation. It is not just what we tell our children that influences their behaviour, but also what they see modelled day after day. If we parents are living with unforgiving judgments in our hearts, our children will perceive our attitudes. My wife, Sherry, reminds me of this when I have at times expressed negative attitudes toward our federal government in the presence of our children. Not long afterwards, we heard those same judgments coming out of our children's mouths.

Theory of Behaviour Change

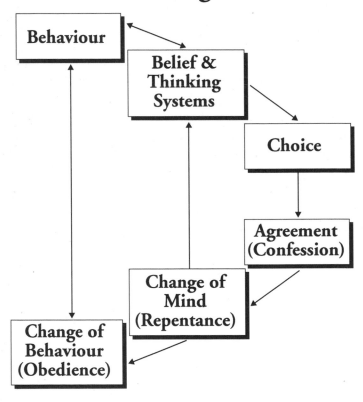

Chapter 18

Forgiveness Is a Choice

The only way to stop being a perpetual victim to someone's sin is to realize that forgiveness is a choice. Nobody ever has to be trapped by somebody else's offences, unless he chooses to live that way. In fact, life offers a series of never-ending choices. I believe this truth passionately (although I don't always live it out). My counselling is based on this premise. The fact that each of us can make choices for ill or for good is what life comprises. My Theory of Behaviour Change diagram serves as an illustration of the importance of choice in forgiveness, and also enables us to see something more of the process of forgiveness as it works in our lives.

Behaviourism

The first part of my theory resulted from the teaching that my mentor, Duane Harder, gave me. Anyone who has studied the psychology of counselling knows there are many theories of counselling. One of the most popular theories is the humanistic theory of behaviourism. Behaviourism implies that people can change who they are by changing individual behaviours, one at a time. For example, if a person is afraid of snakes and wants to overcome that fear, he can be systematically desensitized from the fear of snakes. By taking small, graduated steps, any fear can be eliminated. Change the stimulus, and you can change the response. Add reinforcers or introduce punishment, and you can change the results of specific behaviours. Clearly, there is some measure of truth to this theory. The problem is, we human beings are much more than the sum of our behaviours. We have emotions, a will, a mind and a spirit, as well.

Cognitive psychology

Theorists in the field of counselling eventually recognized that behaviourism as a theory was limited. As a result, cognitive theories became popular. The basic premise of cognitive theories is that all behaviours are predicated on a belief or thinking system. We behave because of what we believe. The way I think determines the way I behave. The values we hold cause the behaviours we exhibit. Counselling theories such as Albert Ellis' Rational Emotive Therapy and Fritz Perls' Gestalt Therapy are typical of this system of belief. When one is able to change an irrational thinking system, one can then improve one's behaviour. To my way of thinking, this was good progress toward the way the real world functioned, but the theory didn't go far enough. Indeed, to change behaviour more permanently, one must change one's belief system. However, I believe there is more.

Responsibility or irresponsibility

Where do the belief systems of individuals come from? Belief systems are acquired through a series of choices made throughout life. Ultimately, we choose what to believe. Otherwise, we become puppets of our parents' thinking, or of the religious or societal upbringing we received. Without choice, we are victims of a system over which we have no control. If that is the case, counselling would be unnecessary. The role of the counsellor is to facilitate change in a person, but change would be impossible if we were stuck in an unchanging system. Choice allows people to take responsibility for both themselves and their behaviours. Who we are largely results from choices we have made. This changes the paradigm from blame to responsibility. William Glasser, in his Reality Therapy, postulates that no such thing as mental illness exists. His theory states that life offers choices between responsibility and irresponsibility. While his theory might seem stark and harsh, it raises a valid point. If I am responsible for who I have become, then I can also change my life through responsibility. All of us can change through making right choices and going in the right direction.

Revelation

To make right choices we must be able to perceive what is the right choice. In psychology this is referred to as insight. Scripture calls it revelation. Unless we have a revelation of the truth, or an awareness of God's perspective, we will live in an assumption of the truth. We will continue to live in the lies we believe in the present. So, for change to occur in our thinking and behaviours, we must see truth as God sees it. Revelation of God's truth, by the Holy Spirit, is always the starting point. As evangelicals we stand for truth as revealed in the Bible. But in order to interpret the Bible correctly, we need the Holy Spirit. In John 16:13–14 Jesus said, 'But when he, the Spirit of truth, comes, he will guide you into all truth. He will not speak on his own; he will speak only what he hears, and he will tell you what is yet to come. He will bring glory to me by taking from what is mine and making it known to you.' Likewise, in counselling a counsellor cannot proceed any further with a client than he or she sees. Moving forward in counselling requires revelation; or, at least, insight. Thus, the Holy Spirit, who leads us into all truth, is called the Counsellor.

Confession

If choice is significant to our identity and belief system, then real change in behaviour and attitudes begins with acknowledging truth. The biblical term is 'confession'. God's Word declares that all men and women have sinned and fallen short of the glory of God. Therefore, we can make changes in our lives by agreeing with God's assessment. The New Testament Greek word for confession is *homolegeo*, which means 'to agree with'. Change begins with a confession to God: 'Where I am today results from choices I made or lies I believed in my past.' Confession of this revealed truth propels us forward in our quest for change. Alcoholics Anonymous came to this conclusion many years ago. They have helped countless people through their Twelve Step programme. The first step in helping people overcome being victims of alcoholism is for them to acknowledge that they are in this predicament because of choices they have made.

I always try to bring people to this same conclusion in the counselling process. Where you are today is because of choices you made. Yet whenever I put this reasoning to people, invariably I am asked this question: 'What about a three-year-old, sexually abused by a father or uncle? Did that child have a choice? Isn't this child a true victim?' My answer to that question is a definite yes and no! In other words, this question is not easy to answer. Obviously, a child's choice at three years of age is very limited. At age five or six, the child may have more choice in the abusive relationship; but still, her choice is limited, because she wants her daddy's acceptance so badly. Even for a ten-year-old, the choices are severely limited. But when a sexually abused person reaches her adolescent or young adult years, she now has a choice. The choice is between retaining bitterness for the wrongful behaviour forced on her, or choosing to forgive and walk free. The assault against her was terribly wrong, but she doesn't have to suffer as a victim of her past for the rest of her life. Forgiveness is a choice that can release a person from continuing as a victim.

It is important to note at this point in the discussion that victims of any kind of abuse do need to grieve the loss of their innocence. What was done to the victim is terribly wrong and the pain needs to be properly acknowledged. Grief is a form of anger. Any time we lose something valuable, we are angry at the loss. Loss is danger to us. Anger forms automatically over our loss. Grief is the word that we use to understand anger arising from loss. To properly grieve a loss, the person must work out their anger from the bereavement they experienced. Although forgiveness appears costly to the victim in working out her anger, it pays off significantly in the end. It is the only way a victim can truly leave the past behind.

Repentance

Having come to the place of confession, the next step in finding freedom is the ability to change one's thinking. In the Bible this is called repentance. For many people the word 'repentance' stirs up thoughts of strange religious people displaying signs saying 'Repent, for the end has come!' To them, the word 'repent' has a negative connotation. But in fact it doesn't mean anything of the kind. The New Testament Greek word for 'repent' is *metanoeo*. It is made up of two Greek words, *meta* (which means 'to change') and *nous* (which means 'the mind'). So, repentance simply means to change the mind, to change the direction of one's thinking. If my thinking has gone in one direction but I repent, my thinking then goes in the opposite direction. To describe it another way, repentance is changing from believing the lie to believing the truth. Knowing and practising that truth has been the most freeing thing I have learned in the past twenty-five years of my life. I am deeply grateful to my pastor, Duane Harder, for teaching me this truth. I know I must choose between the lie and the truth. This has been transforming wisdom for me, personally.

I recognized that my life's previous direction was based on a series of lies that I believed in the past. Once I understood the truth of repentance, I could recognize the lie, confess it, then turn from the lie to the truth. Every time the Holy Spirit showed me another lie, I could follow the same pattern and repent of the lie. The result was that my life shifted from the direction in which the lies took it, to the direction of the truth. Jesus said, 'Then you will know the truth and the truth will set you free' (John 8:32). If we want to be free, we must come to the truth. Where the lies have come from doesn't matter. Whether they come from your culture, your religious background or your upbringing is immaterial. If it is a lie, it is a lie! If you want to know the truth, the Holy Spirit is only too glad to show you the truth through God's Word. In Acts 5:31 and 11:18, we are told it is God who grants us repentance. Repentance is a gift from the Holy Spirit that enables us to change.

Obedience

Confession and repentance are wonderful truths. We don't have to be victims of our past for the rest of our lives. However, once we have made the choice toward repentance, obedience must follow. When we obey what we know is true, we begin making changes in our habits. In the Theory of Behaviour Change diagram, I have noted that when we repent of a lie we have believed, we make both long-term and short-term changes. Repentance changes our overall belief system but also changes our immediate behaviour. Of course, the opposite is also true. When we continually change our behaviours, we change our belief systems. Many people in counselling originally come with little hope of seeing substantial change in their lives. Although they genuinely want changes, they know they have remained the same for a long time. 'Will I ever be able to make real changes in my life?' they ask. But all change comes one step at a time. When people see a realistic way to make changes, they develop hope and motivation to continue working at it.

Once a man came in to the counselling centre to see me about his marriage. His first question was, 'Do you think it's too late for me to make major changes in my life?' I asked how old he was; he told me he was fifty-four years old. I asked how many good years he thought he had left; he said, possibly twenty or thirty. I told him it is never too late to begin making changes. Why waste the next twenty or thirty years by doing nothing about it now? The longer you wait, the more work is required, but it is never too late to start. He went on to work through some significant issues in his past, and from that work his marriage was restored in ways he never thought possible.

Chapter 19

The Importance of Forgiving Others

I shared my theory of counselling with you because I believe forgiveness comes under the realm of choice. When we understand how destructive bitterness is to us, we must choose either to proceed with working it through or to leave it buried in the past. In an encounter with his disciples, recorded in Luke 17:1–10, Jesus showed clearly how essential forgiveness is:

> *Jesus said to his disciples: 'Things that cause people to sin are bound to come, but woe to that person through whom they come. It would be better for him to be thrown into the sea with a millstone tied around his neck than for him to cause one of these little ones to sin. So watch yourselves.*
>
> *'If your brother sins, rebuke him, and if he repents, forgive him. If he sins against you seven times in a day, and seven times comes back to you and says, "I repent," forgive him.'*
>
> *The apostles said to the Lord, 'Increase our faith!'*
>
> *He replied, 'If you have faith as small as a mustard seed, you can say to this mulberry tree, "Be uprooted and planted in the sea," and it will obey you.*
>
> *'Suppose one of you had a servant ploughing or looking after the sheep. Would he say to the servant when he comes in from the field, "Come along now and sit down*

*to eat"? Would he not rather say, "Prepare my supper,
get yourself ready and wait on me while I eat and drink;
after that you may eat and drink"? Would he thank the
servant because he did what he was told to do? So you
also, when you have done everything you were told to do,
should say, "We are unworthy servants; we have only
done our duty."'*

In Luke, Jesus says that you have not done a great thing
in forgiving your brother over and over again. You have
only done your duty. You have done what is expected.
Just as you have been forgiven but didn't deserve it, so
your forgiveness of others isn't because they deserve
to be forgiven. Because we received mercy, we extend
mercy. As we received forgiveness, we extend forgiveness
(Colossians 3:13). As we received God's grace (his power
and presence), so we extend his grace to others around us.
We are to function with a servant attitude. Our Christian
duty is to forgive. Forgiveness is commanded; it is not a
benevolent extra that demonstrates our spiritual maturity.
Just as the natural response of a servant is to serve, so also
the natural response of a Christian is to forgive. When we
forgive our brother (or sister) seventy times seven, we
have only fulfilled our basic duty. When we are faced with
the truth of these scriptures, we realize we have a choice.
Will we forgive or hold on to our grudges?

Perhaps you are thinking, 'That's easy for you to say,
making forgiveness so black and white, Graham. If you
knew what I've been through and how greatly I have been
hurt, you wouldn't be so dogmatic.' I agree that forgiveness
is difficult to work through when we are deeply wounded.
However, for us to put our circumstances above the
truth of God's Word is dangerous. Nothing is impossible
with God. God gives grace for forgiveness, which can be

learned. So the next step in this process is to reveal how forgiveness is learned.

Forgiveness can be learned

Step 1: Begin with a realization of your own mistakes

Who of us hasn't hurt others and caused offence? In John 8, Jesus said to the crowd who were ready to stone the woman caught in adultery, 'If any one of you is without sin, let him be the first to throw a stone at her.' He was telling us something we already know intuitively. None of us is sinless. All of us have hurt others as much as we have been hurt. Everyone is on the same level. When we examine our own sins and mistakes, we are humbled because we know we are not perfect and never can be. When we have a revelation of our imperfections, we are not so quick to condemn others for the very sins we ourselves have committed.

Step 2: Consider the pain of not being forgiven for your mistakes

How would you like to go through life without forgiveness for all the mistakes you made and sins you committed? Jesus said in Matthew 7:12, 'Do unto others as you would have them do unto you.' We call this the 'golden rule' because we recognize the wisdom of living this way. We know we can't bear guilt for long. We don't want to be burdened with the weight and pressure of unforgiven sin, either. In fact, the pressure of unresolved guilt has put many people into mental institutions. The pressure was too great to bear. Only arrogant men or women proudly proclaim that they don't need forgiveness.

Step 3: Realize that what you expect from others should be given to others

If we expect others to forgive us when we fail or sin against them, we should see the logic of treating others the same way. Jesus tells a powerful story in Matthew 18 of a man who owed his king millions of dollars. When he couldn't pay his debt, he was hauled before the king to give an account for what he owed. He pleaded with the king to give him more time (which was ridiculous, considering the amount he owed). However, the king had mercy on him and forgave his enormous debt. Shortly afterward, this same servant saw a fellow servant who owed him about twenty dollars. He grabbed the man by the throat and demanded instant repayment of this small amount. When the man also asked for a short extension to pay, the first servant threw him into debtors' prison. When the king heard how the first servant had treated his fellow servant, he was furious. He rescinded his earlier order of debt forgiveness and threw the unforgiving man in jail until every last penny was paid. Then Jesus gave us this warning: 'This is how my heavenly Father will treat each of you unless you forgive your brother from your heart.'

Step 4: Extend the same attitude to those who have offended you

Since we already have been forgiven so much by God, it only makes sense that we should be willing to forgive others who offend us. This is not only the teaching of Scripture, but also it is a logical argument. However, having had to deal with my own unforgiveness, and that of many others in counselling, I realize that, through the emotional reaction of hurt, this logic often escapes us. Nevertheless, we should admit that even in the world's way of thinking, this logic is very persuasive.

Step 5: Forgiveness frees you to enjoy life again and is well worth the investment

The freedom we experience in releasing and forgiving someone's wrong against us is well worth whatever effort we expend to overcome our hurt and pain. By forgiving others, we are preparing the ground for the seed of forgiveness when we ourselves will need it. Whoever, past or present, has hurt us, must be forgiven from the heart. When they are set free, each of us will live in that same freedom.

The power of forgiveness to transform a life

A woman, whom we'll call Daphne, came into my counselling office for a consultation. Daphne came because she had recently read a newspaper article about a woman who had successfully prosecuted a man who had sexually abused her as a child. This abuse had occurred twenty-five years earlier. After Daphne had read this article, she went to the police and wrote out a twelve-page, detailed affidavit charging the man who had abused her twenty-eight years earlier. Daphne was a professional woman but when I first met her, I would not have known that to look at her. She was dressed in sweatpants and a sweatshirt, and her hair was uncared for. She had no make-up and looked depressed and exhausted. Daphne told me she was on a leave of absence from her job because she had become so stressed about what had happened to her all those years ago. I read the police report that she had written out and then she filled in more details.

When Daphne was ten years old, her sister's boyfriend, then eighteen, began having intercourse with her. This happened regularly for a year. Daphne and I speculated that he stopped because her mother was suspicious. He was afraid of getting caught and sent to jail. Daphne was verbally threatened by this man and sworn to secrecy, so she told no one. Daphne never shared this experience of abuse with anyone until six years later. When she was sixteen, Daphne's doctor gave her an internal physical examination. He said to her, 'You've had intercourse, haven't you?' He made a note in her medical files. She told the doctor her whole story, but he said he couldn't do much about it, because it had happened six years earlier.

At twenty-two years of age, Daphne married, but the marriage broke up in a few years because she had difficulty with sexual intimacy. When they went through counselling to try saving their marriage, she shared her story with their counsellor. The counsellor's response was the same as the doctor's. It happened too long ago for any justice to be worked out, so leave it alone. By the time she came to see me, she was thirty-eight years old. This meant that the sexual abuse had occurred twenty-eight years ago. Anger had burned in her for that length of time. Now the accumulated internal stress was too much for her and she was falling apart emotionally and physically. (This experience is commonly referred to as a nervous breakdown.)

What Daphne needed from the counselling was emotional readiness to face the court case that was coming in a few months. I told Daphne that I saw nothing wrong with pursuing justice against this man. However, I told her that justice would not free her from the deep anger she carried toward him. In her view, the only way she could get free of this blight was to charge the man and see him given jail time. I gently suggested to Daphne that justice would never give back her lost years. Only forgiveness would free her to go on with life. (I'm sure at that point she thought my psychologist's licence wasn't worth the paper it was written on.) We debated this choice between justice and forgiveness for two counselling sessions before she finally saw what I was saying and agreed to try working out her anger through forgiveness.

I began using the Forgiveness Exercise (see Appendix 3). Daphne worked diligently at her homework. She began to sense this might work, even though it was hard for her. She shed a lot of tears over it. One day, after six months of meeting weekly, Daphne came to see me. She was full of anger and was expressing it in no uncertain terms. We knew the court date had already been set and it was to be held in a city in central Canada where she had grown up (and where this man still lived). However, her abuser, through his lawyer, had manipulated the court system through a technicality to delay the case several months. Daphne was livid – she was so angry, she was 'spitting nails'. I had been counselling her that justice (and revenge) would not satisfy her longing to be healed. I had also told her that if she lost the court case, she would be angrier than ever. Now that the justice system seemed to have failed her, she recognized that she needed to do more work to forgive this man for his crime against her.

We continued for two more months, until Daphne felt the anger lift from her. About that time she came for her last few appointments. When I went to the front office to greet her, I hardly recognized her. Her hair was styled nicely and she wore make-up. She was dressed in a business suit and looked very smart. I said to her jokingly, 'Have I met you before?' I told her that it was obvious that she had 'turned the corner' and was on her way to freedom. After two more counselling sessions, we completed our work; I didn't hear anything more from her for a while. Two years later, a friend of mine was delivering a seminar in another Canadian city. Daphne had organized this seminar through the company where she worked. During the seminar, my counsellor friend talked about forgiveness. This subject triggered powerful memories for Daphne. At the end of the day, she asked the speaker if he knew me, as we were from the same city. When she found that he did, she sent a note with him, telling me that she was doing well and that she felt like a new woman. I never learned the outcome of the court case.

Daphne's life presents a real story both of forgiveness and of the transformation forgiveness brings when people work it through faithfully. Stories like hers bring hope to others. Nobody has to remain a victim for the rest of his or her life. Freedom is a choice derived through forgiveness. I love helping people choose forgiveness and freedom, then watching the resulting changes.

Chapter 20
The Forgiveness Exercise

Through years of helping people overcome buried anger, I wrestled with the need for a practical tool to help them work out anger. I experimented with a number of tools. Finally I developed an exercise that has proved immensely useful to me and to my clients. You, the reader, can use this exercise to help you discover the power of forgiveness. I have included my Forgiveness Exercise at the end of this book (see Appendix 3). I now want to go through this exercise, step by step, in order to make it usable for you. This is an amazingly simple way of helping people work through hurt, pain and bitterness. I have used the Forgiveness Exercise repeatedly to help my clients work through their buried anger. It is not a self-help exercise but one that can be used by counsellors and others trained to help people find freedom. Although you don't need to be a psychologist, professional counsellor or social worker to be able to use this tool, you need careful instruction and guidance from the Holy Spirit in order to use it effectively.

Step 1: List the people you need to forgive

The first step in the exercise is to write down the names of the people you need to forgive. List those people who have hurt you the most, or have failed you in some significant way. Both parents are usually key people, along with siblings, other relatives, teachers, pastors, or whoever else has wounded you. I usually don't ask people to list all the people who have wounded them but rather the significant people (three to five people is common). Often, one particular person is the most significant offender. Therefore, the majority of time is centred on him or her.

Step 2: Recognize how bitterness is self-destructive

If you bury negative feelings you have toward yourself and others, you will inevitably engage in some form of self-destructive behaviour. In this step, write down behaviours you engage in that hurt you. For example, eating problems caused by buried anger are self-destructive. Whether you are over-eating or under-eating, you are hurting yourself by that behaviour. If you are dealing with stored anger by drinking too much alcohol, you are hurting yourself. Other self-destructive behaviours include over-exercising, or never exercising, using drugs, demeaning yourself through personal criticism, chewing your fingernails or withdrawing from relationships. Write down anything you do that you think may result from stored anger energy in you.

Stored anger often produces anxiety, which causes you to hurt yourself or others. I have known people who dealt with buried anger through addiction to television. Their lives are controlled by the television and they do not realize what is causing their addiction. I take people through this step to help increase their motivation for forgiving others. Sometimes anger is so great that you don't have motivation for working through forgiveness. However, when you discover the connection between buried anger and self-destructive behaviour, you may decide that 'enough is enough'. Why destroy yourself through something destructive that happened to you in the past? Why allow yourself to be victimized twice? The first time, you may not have had a choice in the matter. But if you retain anger and it becomes bitterness, you become a victim all over again.

Step 3: Describe briefly what happened

The third step is to list all the incidents in which you were hurt by this person. I don't mean every detail of each event must be written out. I usually ask the person to make a brief note of the incident so we can discuss it further in the counselling session. You must work through one person at a time, because attempting several people at once causes confusion. (For example, you can start with your father.) These incidents may be specific things that your father did or said to you. They may include words your father never said to you (e.g. he never told you that he loved you). They may include general attitudes your father has had about you (e.g. you'll never amount to anything). They may also include what your father failed to do for you (e.g. he never came to see your ball games). They may include promises made and broken or unrealistic expectations that were held over you. I ask people to list all the hurts from their father. Some people like working chronologically. Other people like listing from memory whatever comes to mind at the time. I suggest that people pray, asking the Holy Spirit for help in remembering key incidents from long ago.

My goal is not to blame fathers or any other person. Blaming is a useless exercise. Blaming indicates that we still have significant buried anger in ourselves. Our goal is to communicate honestly about where you hurt so that you can discover where buried anger is located in your heart.

Step 4: Identify the emotions involved

In Step 4 you are to identify the emotions that comprise the pain of your past. You have to feel in order to heal. We experience the pain of hurt and rejection in our emotions. To try to remain objective or emotionally removed while doing this exercise is a waste of time. When you were deeply hurt by the person you are trying to forgive, the hurt was not felt in your brain or your mind. The hurt was felt or experienced in your emotions. That is why you must identify the emotions you felt at the time of your pain. At the beginning of the exercise, you listed, objectively, what was done to you that caused great hurt. But in Step 4, you must engage your emotions.

I realize this process causes great discomfort and sometimes deep anguish for the people I work with. I have been asked, 'Why must I re-live the pain of the past? Wasn't it enough that I went through that once before?' This aspect is the most difficult thing I ask of people going through the exercise. But I have also found that avoiding the pain of the past minimizes the release of forgiveness. This is the only way that I have found to release the deep pain. You must confront the pain by touching it again. So, Step 4 involves going back in your memory to the first event listed in Step 3, identifying the emotions you went through at the time you were hurt. For example, if you were hurt by your father's constant criticism, you might have felt unaccepted by him, angry at his constant judgments and helpless because you didn't know how to gain his acceptance. It is not the words you put on paper that are important but the experience of re-living that pain.

The purpose of Step 4 is to draw the poison out, touching the pain of buried anger. (I suggest these words be written in the margin beside the event listed or, perhaps, written in red ink so that the words are seen easily.)

I have discovered, in going through this exercise, that many people find that the words 'I forgive you' are not enough. Without the release of pain and buried anger, forgiveness does not actually take effect. By releasing anger, we experience the release of forgiveness. Writing down our experiences works like a poultice to draw out the poison of bitterness. The slow, systematic work of writing pulls out anger and then the forgiveness is completed. In the counselling session we talk about what was written by the client, which further releases anger from the person.

Step 5: Express your hurt and anger by writing a letter to the offender

Once you have connected your hurt and pain to your desire to forgive, you must take another step in the direction of removing your anger. I call this step the 'anger letter'. This letter is designed to tell the offender exactly what you think of him in your anger. In other words, you will 'tell him off'. However, it must be done in a therapeutically controlled environment. This letter is not done for revenge but for release. If the letter were ever sent to the offender it would be received as revenge. If you were to show someone the letter it would act as gossip. The only persons who see the letter should be you and your counsellor, pastor or whomever you have chosen to help you. This letter is not to be used to confront your offender. Its sole purpose is to release stored past anger and present anger so that you can fully forgive. (The letter should be given only to the counsellor helping you through this exercise. They should hold it in their files so that no one else sees it.)

To be effective, this anger letter must be an 'angry' letter, not a 'nice' one. Sometimes, when people do this exercise, they write a nice letter. So I return it, asking them to write an 'angry' letter instead. I say to them, 'However you express yourself when you are truly angry, is what I want you to write. Don't write this letter to please me or so that I won't think badly about you.' Because I'm not only a psychologist but also a pastor, people often tone down the language they use. I tell them to use the language they would use in their anger, but I forbid them to take the Lord's name in vain. That's my only stipulation, because I don't want to bring God's judgment on them. It's not that I want to promote the use of 'barnyard' language, but neither do I want to restrict people from venting their true feelings of anger. However you release anger when you experience rage is what I am seeking. That's what this part of the exercise is all about. Hopefully your counsellor, who alone will see your letter, will not be offended by 'expressive' language.

Sometimes, I find that people need to begin their letters with, 'Dear Dad [or whoever], you know I love you and appreciate you, but…' Then they feel free to confront the person with the areas in which he has failed and hurt them. It is the people we love the most who often hurt us the most. Keeping anger stored in our emotions only serves to alienate us from those we love. So, affirm your loyalty and love but get on with the process of releasing your anger.

Step 6: Cancel the debt

When you have released the other person from your own expectations, you are ready to forgive – to cancel the debt. Forgiveness as a decision means choosing not to hold on to an emotional 'debt' against another person. Forgiveness as a process means working through your own inner reactions until what was done to you no longer dominates you or causes you pain and hurt. Cancelling the debt means acknowledging your hurt yet choosing to release the person from what they have done. If you are unwilling to cancel the debt by forgiving, you continue to remain a victim.

Sometimes people tell me that forgiveness is extremely difficult. I ask if they have reached a decision to forgive. They are unsure they want to forgive. So, I ask if they are willing to start the process of working out their anger. Once they start the process, the decision to proceed through to forgiveness often follows. As anger is released, the decision to forgive becomes easier. Other times, the motivation to work on the process is halted because there has been no internal decision to forgive. At such times, they must decide what they are going to do with their anger, or the process of forgiveness will not work for them.

Sometimes, people write out their forgiveness statement and read it to me. Most times, they choose to express it in the form of prayer. Remember, the decision to forgive is yours. Nobody can choose it for you. You have the power to forgive or to withhold forgiveness. I ask people to specifically include in their prayer the words, 'I forgive...' (mentioning the name of their offender). Whenever a person releases forgiveness through prayer, I commonly pray a prayer of release over the counsellee. As a counsellor, I want to be present to hear or read the prayers of forgiveness because of the peace it brings to the person who is praying with me. The Bible commands us to forgive as we have been forgiven (Ephesians 4:32). Once we have forgiven, a great weight is lifted from our shoulders, giving our souls peace. Releasing people from the debt they owe is the natural response to having our own debts cancelled by God.

Step 7: Consider the possibility of reconciliation

In this step, you must distinguish between forgiveness and reconciliation. Forgiveness is a one-way street whereas reconciliation is a two-way street. This is a very important distinction! People sometimes think forgiveness means automatic reconciliation. This misconception causes them to withhold forgiveness. But I am adamant that a person should not be forced to return to a relationship where both sides of the offence have not been resolved. To send a person back into relationship with an offender who has not acknowledged his abuse, is dangerous and wrong. The offended person is positioned for more abuse. Where trust has been violated, there is no easy way to rebuild trust. Clearly, the first step in rebuilding trust is the prevention of continuing offences. If the offender acknowledges his wrong and truly repents, then reconciliation has potential. You never can force reconciliation between persons, but it is always an excellent goal to aim for, if it is workable. It is especially desirable in marriage conflicts, since the marriage cannot last for long without reconciliation.

In the Forgiveness Exercise, I have included a series of questions that I encourage each person to ask himself or herself:

- Why is this reconciliation important to you?

- Work through what you think his/her response will be.

- Can you find out if this person is open to working through his/her part of the reconciliation process?

- Can you accept a rejection response from this person?

Working through these questions enables you to see where reconciliation may or may not be possible. However, forgiveness always brings freedom to you, even without reconciliation. Unfortunately, in a sinful world, some relationships are irreconcilable.

The difficult part of any reconciliation is learning to trust again. In a relationship, trust requires a long time to build yet a short time to destroy. Every married couple knows the pain of hurting one's spouse and the days, or even weeks and months that are necessary to rebuild trust in the damaged area of the relationship. To reconcile and enjoy trust in the relationship again is virtually impossible without working through forgiveness thoroughly. In 2 Corinthians 5:18–19 Paul tells us that Christians have the 'ministry of reconciliation'. The text says God first reconciled sinful human beings to himself through Christ's atoning sacrifice on the cross. Then he gave this same ministry of reconciliation to all Christians to help others be reconciled to God, as well. However, to engage in this ministry of reconciliation to the world is not realistic without living in reconciliation as Christians with our brothers and sisters in Christ. So, as much as possible, Christians must work toward reconciliation with those who have hurt and angered them. That is why the work of forgiveness is so basic and essential to both our lives and our lifestyle. Genuine forgiveness is the only way for trust to be re-established in broken relationships.

Chapter 21

A Biblical View of Forgiveness

The Bible, in particular the New Testament, teaches extensively on forgiveness, which is one of the fundamentals of the faith. To experience forgiveness personally is to experience God. In fact, the only way any sinful, broken human being can experience the reality of God's love is first through receiving his forgiveness. The basic need for forgiveness arises because God is holy and we humans are rebellious and sinful.

One of the most graphic illustrations I have seen of this truth is in the classic movie, *Raiders of the Lost Ark*. In the film, Indiana Jones has been pursuing the prize of the lost Ark of the Covenant, fighting the Nazis every step of the way. He and his girlfriend, Marion, are captured, once again, on a desert island and tied together to a post. The Nazis, who have no sense of the 'holy' whatsoever, finally decide to open the captured Ark. As the lid of the Ark is opened, a sweeping power is released from the box. The presence and power of God's holiness destroys everything in its path, annihilating all the people who dared to look. The profane is destroyed by the sacred. Sinful people are eradicated by the sinless presence of a holy God. Indiana Jones is wise enough to cover his eyes, not looking on the presence of this holy God as the Ark is opened. The Nazis are destroyed while Indiana and Marion are saved from the awesome and destructive power of the holy. This graphic picture is exactly what would happen if we, as sinners, ever tried to enter God's presence while in our sinful state. In Exodus 33:20 God tells Moses, 'you cannot see my face, for no one may see me and live.'

The impossible gap

Without forgiveness, relationship with God is impossible. God's holiness separates him from us because we are unholy. Because God is holy and sinless and we are rebellious and sinful, God devised a plan to bridge the 'impossible' gap. Jesus, God's Son (equal with the Father), left the glory of heaven, and became human to become the sin-bearer. God, the Father, devised a plan whereby his sinless Son would atone for our sins. In order to bridge the gap between rebellious man and sinless God, God's anger and justice must be appeased. That is why God released the full fury of his wrath on Jesus at the cross. God allowed Satan and sinful people to do whatever they wanted to Jesus in his torture and death. But (and this is a big BUT!) God raised Jesus from the dead and triumphed over Satan, sin, death and hell. All we need is to receive what God did for us in Christ's death on the cross. If we believe, we can receive. Forgiveness is free because Jesus paid for it with his life.

That is why forgiveness is central to the Bible's message of salvation. To forgive all those who have hurt us is crucial. Ephesians 4:32 says: 'Be kind and compassionate to one another, forgiving each other, just as in Christ God forgave you.' Forgiving others is how we continually thank God for forgiving us. When we consistently fail to forgive others who have wronged us, we misunderstand what it cost God the Father and God the Son to forgive us.

Unconditional forgiveness?

In Matthew 6, Jesus teaches his disciples about giving, praying and fasting. A parallel passage in Luke 11 suggests that this teaching was a response to a request by the disciples: 'Teach us to pray.' Jesus led his disciples through five keys of prayer: worship, intercession, petition, forgiveness and protection. (By the way, it was not meant to be a memorized prayer but a teaching tool on how to pray.) Interestingly, Jesus' only commentary on this brief teaching on prayer is about forgiveness. Forgiveness is so essential to effective prayer that Jesus emphasizes it by this statement: 'For if you forgive men when they sin against you, your heavenly Father will also forgive you. But if you do not forgive men their sins, your Father will not forgive your sins' (Matthew 6:14–15). I admit that for years I found a great deal of difficulty in understanding these two verses.

I was taught in theological college that God's forgiveness is unconditional. But Jesus has a condition for receiving God's forgiveness. He says, if you want to be forgiven, you must forgive others. What exactly is Jesus telling us? Scripture teaches that God's forgiveness is both unconditional, yet conditional. If we ask in faith for God to forgive us, through confessing and repenting of our sins, inviting Jesus to become Lord of our lives, he will. It is as simple as that! Theologians call this 'positional' truth. We can count on it and stand on it because God always keeps his word. When we surrender control of our lives to Jesus, we are born from above or 'born again' and forgiven (John 3:1–8). However, if we want to experience God's forgiveness, we must live our faith by forgiving others. So many Christians miss the power of the Holy Spirit in their lives because they are filled with bitterness toward other people. They cannot live as forgiven people because they refuse to forgive others.

Will God retract his forgiveness from us once he has given it to us? No, I don't believe God will do that, because he established a covenant of forgiveness with us through his Son, Jesus. To take away our forgiveness would nullify everything that Christ accomplished both in his death on the cross and in his resurrection from the dead. However, we nullify the power of Christ's forgiveness in our lives by withholding forgiveness from others.

Forgiving ourselves

A second issue is intertwined in this process of giving and receiving forgiveness. Many times I have heard people tell me the importance of forgiving themselves. The concept intrigued me, but is it biblically true? I searched the Scriptures in vain, to find any verses of instruction to forgive ourselves. I found no expression of that concept in the Bible. Although I understand what people mean in suggesting we forgive ourselves, theologically it is incorrect, and realistically, it is impossible to do. Let me explain.

Imagine you have been caught speeding by the police. You have been given a traffic ticket for going well beyond the speed limit. You do not really want to pay the fine so you go to court to fight the ticket. As you stand before the judge, you ask if you can speak in your own defence. You tell the judge that, although you know you are guilty of breaking the speed limit, you have decided to forgive yourself. The judge looks at you as if you have lost your mind. 'I'm sorry,' says his Honour, 'but you don't have authority to forgive your own traffic ticket. I'm the one who has been given the authority to determine guilt versus innocence, and I find you guilty.'

That is the same issue that we face when we try to forgive ourselves for our sins or our mistakes. I believe that what these well-meaning people are trying to say is that we need to learn to receive our forgiveness from God. God the Judge grants us pardon for our sins because his Son, Jesus, paid for 'our ticket'. Our part is learning to truly receive the forgiveness we are given. Receiving forgiveness is more difficult than people realize.

Jesus tells a very powerful story in Matthew 18:21–35 to illustrate the difference between those who truly receive forgiveness and those who only think they have.

Receiving forgiveness from God

Then Peter came to Jesus and asked, 'Lord, how many times shall I forgive my brother when he sins against me? Up to seven times?'

Jesus answered, 'I tell you, not seven times, but seventy-seven times.

'Therefore, the kingdom of heaven is like a king who wanted to settle accounts with his servants. As he began the settlement, a man who owed him ten thousand talents was brought to him. Since he was not able to pay, the master ordered that he and his wife and his children and all that he had be sold to repay the debt.

'The servant fell on his knees before him. "Be patient with me," he begged, "and I will pay back everything." The servant's master took pity on him, cancelled the debt and let him go.

'But when that servant went out, he found one of his fellow servants who owed him a hundred denarii. He grabbed him and began to choke him. "Pay back what you owe me!" he demanded.

'His fellow servant fell to his knees and begged him,

"Be patient with me, and I will pay you back."

'But he refused. Instead, he went off and had the man thrown into prison until he could pay the debt. When the other servants saw what had happened, they were greatly distressed and went and told their master everything that had happened.

'Then the master called the servant in. "You wicked servant," he said, "I cancelled all that debt of yours because you begged me to. Shouldn't you have had mercy on your fellow servant just as I had on you?" In anger his master turned him over to the jailers to be tortured, until he should pay back all he owed.

'This is how my heavenly Father will treat each of you unless you forgive your brother from your heart.'

Forgiveness is so basic to the Christian faith that most understand it. Nevertheless, unforgiveness remains a great stumbling block to the release of the Holy Spirit's power in the church today. In counselling over the years, particularly with Christians, I am still amazed at how many people are not operating in the freedom of forgiveness. This was the case with a pastor who was leading a successful church but was struggling with conflict with members of his staff. In sharing his story with the counsellor, he revealed a debilitating problem in his life. As a result of insecurity, he felt compelled to be right, all the time. This pride led to conflict with other staff members. Then the counsellor discovered unresolved sexual sins, including an ongoing battle with pornography. The pastor was deeply ashamed of his moral failure. A significant part of his struggle was his inability to receive forgiveness from God for his sins, particularly this weakness with pornography. His struggles were rooted in bitterness he still retained toward his father and mother. When he humbly opened his heart to resolve the unforgiveness toward his family, he was freed from his past and also had victory in his battle with pornography.

Why didn't the king's servant forgive?

For years I have read and understood the basic message of Matthew 18: If we are forgiven, we must forgive. But I was puzzled by this question: Why didn't the first servant forgive his fellow servant, considering the overwhelming circumstances of his own forgiveness by the king? Doesn't it make sense to forgive someone a few dollars when he was forgiven millions?

To understand what's in this Scripture passage, let's first address some basic issues: the forgiveness of God is free, yet it's not free; it's an unconditional offer, yet it has a condition; there are no strings attached, yet there's a string! Are we communicating, yet? Sounds confusing, doesn't it? Once you receive forgiveness, which is free, you are required to extend forgiveness to others, which is a condition. This is exactly what Jesus said in Matthew 6:14–15: 'For if you forgive men when they sin against you, your heavenly Father will also forgive you. But if you do not forgive men their sins, your Father will not forgive your sins.' However, a vast difference exists between being offered forgiveness and being able to receive it. The first servant was offered forgiveness – a complete pardon – and it looked like he had received it. Yet, as the story tells us in the end, he did not actually receive his pardon. Let's examine the process of forgiveness for some clues which explain this enigma.

We must realize our need of forgiveness

In verse 23, the king calls attention to the outstanding

debt owed by the servant. Seemingly, the servant did not realize he owed the king money. How is this possible, you say? He owed millions of dollars. Obviously, he was living in denial. He must have known he owed a huge sum, but perhaps he was hoping his account wouldn't be called up. Do people really live like this? Just look around you and you see it all the time. In counselling, I see it on a regular basis. When people bring a certain problem, I realize that there must have been an extensive and unresolved history for the problem to exist. Our most frequent defence mechanism to avoid reality is denial. And this servant was living in the midst of unreality. But now, this man is called to account, to face his debt. He needs forgiveness in a major way.

We will be confronted by the King (the Holy Spirit)

Sooner or later, we will be confronted by the 'debt' of sin we have accumulated. It is as inevitable as death and taxes, as they say. During the holiday season, drivers may be able to avoid the police check-stops for a time, but sooner or later, when they least expect it, they will run into a roadside check that they can't avoid. The King arranges our circumstances so that we are forced to see the condition of our hearts – to face reality. Sooner or later, God will bring us all to a place of frustration, anguish or pain. Then we will have to examine our hearts and be honest about our sin. The Holy Spirit of God shows us the extent of our debt because of our sin. While we think of it as just a few dollars, the Holy Spirit shows us that in fact it's millions of dollars. Only the Holy Spirit can show us our heart condition and how badly we need to be forgiven.

We must realize that we cannot pay back our debt

If we think we can repay the full amount of our debt in any manner, we are caught in some form of religion. That is exactly what religion is: a system of trying to pay back God for our accumulated debt of sin. Whether in religious pilgrimages, giving money to charity, attending church, helping out by serving the poor, or reading our Bibles more (all of which have their place), any attempt to pay for our sin is futile. The debt load is far too large. As James 2:10 says, 'For whoever keeps the whole law and yet stumbles at just one point is guilty of breaking all of it.' So even if we think we have lived a relatively good life, from God's perspective our rebellion against him makes us as guilty as the worst sinner. One of the most believed lies from Satan is that we can pay God back for our debt of sin. Somehow, we think, we can earn our forgiveness through good deeds for God. Both Christians and non-Christians are duped by this lie many times, as we will see in our story. Believing this very lie keeps many from experiencing true repentance with God. Believing this lie also holds many Christians in a state of powerlessness.

We must cry out for mercy

When the servant heard the king's decree that he and his wife and family were sold into slavery until the debt was paid, he did the only thing he could think of. He cried out for mercy. Verse 26 says this servant fell on his knees before the king and begged for time to pay back his debt. The servant's cry for mercy evoked the king's compassion. He forgave the whole enormous debt. Wow! What amazing love and mercy was shown to the servant! Since the servant couldn't possibly repay the debt, the king's only alternative was to cancel the whole debt. This parable shows exactly what forgiveness is. What changed the king's mind? The king responded to the servant's cry for mercy – not to his statement, 'I will pay everything back.' Full payment was impossible and the king knew it. God always responds to a cry for mercy because he is the God of mercy. For us to think we can pay God back for all of our sins against him is simply ludicrous. The cry, 'Get me out of this one, God, and I'll serve you forever!' doesn't work. Only our cry for mercy receives a response of mercy from him.

We must receive forgiveness in our hearts

In order for forgiveness truly to change us, it must touch our hearts. If our cry of desperation is only a stalling tactic to repay everything, then we will not receive forgiveness in our hearts. This servant did not ultimately receive his forgiveness because he believed he would somehow repay the king. He was still living in denial. He could not possibly repay such a large debt. Let's come back to the question we asked earlier: Why didn't the first servant forgive his fellow servant? The answer is obvious now. He did not forgive his fellow servant because he had not really experienced forgiveness himself. In his heart, he thought he could pay for his own sins; that is, repay the king. So, why shouldn't his fellow servant repay him? Many Christians also think like this. We think it is our right to withhold forgiveness from someone else until they repay us to our expectations. So how do we know we have actually received forgiveness from God? We know by looking for symptoms of unforgiveness in our lives.

Chapter 22
Symptoms of Unforgiveness

Forgiveness, as we know, is an ongoing process in our lives. Even when we are born again of the Spirit of God, not only are we capable of sin but also we do sin. All of us can return to a system of trying to repay God through good behaviour. However, many of us operate as if we were not forgiven by God. Like this servant, we were offered forgiveness from the King, but we have not received it into our hearts. How do we know? We manifest symptoms of unforgiveness, as did the king's servant in this parable. Here are ten symptoms of unforgiveness:

1. A spirit of judgment

Notice the phrase in verse 28, 'he found one of his fellow servants who owed him a hundred denarii'. The servant went looking for his fellow servant because he was still aware of needing money to repay the king. If he could collect from his fellow servant he could use that to repay the king. When we have not received forgiveness from God, we become judgmental and critical of others who have hurt us. In other words, we try to collect from others to pay our debt. We are quick to condemn others because we feel condemned ourselves. We look for faults in people so we can collect from others to remove the pressure from ourselves.

2. Hidden bitterness

In verse 28 we read that when this servant found his fellow servant, 'He grabbed him and began to choke him'. It is obvious that there was a great deal of stored anger in this servant. He not only asked for his money, he 'throttled' his fellow servant. Clearly it was the stored anger and bitterness that caused him to react so violently. When we bury anger toward someone who has offended us, the potential for over-reaction increases greatly.

3. A spirit of unforgiveness

This servant demanded of his fellow servant, 'pay back what you owe me'. There was vindictiveness in his spirit, such that he would not let go of even the smallest offence. Isn't that how we feel when someone hurts us or has something against us? We develop a spirit of unforgiveness so that even small offences cause a reaction in us. Because we have not resolved past areas of offence, the present is often a minefield of explosive incidents that set us off.

4. Lack of love and joy

In this state of unforgiveness, we walk around in a fog, with little enjoyment of life. We become self-focused, not looking out for others or caring about them. Self-protection becomes a way of life. We lack joy and find it hard to love others, especially those who 'bug' us.

5. Abuse of power

Buried anger causes us to strike out at others, sometimes for no apparent reason. We find ourselves wanting to control or hurt others, especially when they arouse our anger. Because of stored anger, we abuse the authority God has given us in our homes, jobs and churches. Even worse, we can't seem to stop ourselves. We act the same as this servant, misusing the power of anger.

6. Lack of experiencing God's presence

When there is bitterness in our hearts, buried anger pushes the presence of Jesus into the background; we act as though Jesus is not living in us. In fact, if we are in this state of bitterness, most people would be surprised to discover we are followers of Jesus, because of how we act. We also cease to function in the grace of God (i.e. his enabling power and presence).

7. Ceaseless activity

In losing the presence and power of God, we substitute activity or Christian service for the real power of God. We 'burn the candle at both ends', not knowing why we do it. Perhaps busyness turns our minds away from our guilty consciences. Or perhaps the enemy keeps us so busy that we won't have time to reflect on the condition of our hearts. An unforgiving heart is a busy heart, and our busyness does not serve the King.

8. Doubt our salvation

Another symptom of an unforgiving heart is a lack of ongoing relationship with Jesus. In counselling, I have noted this disconnection. Christians who carry unforgiveness often doubt their salvation. We wonder whether God could forgive our sins, since we are unwilling to forgive others' sins. We feel unworthy, unloved, angry with ourselves and uncared for by God.

9. Low self-esteem

Uncertainty of God's feelings for us compounds our feelings about ourselves. We dislike ourselves because we don't believe God likes us. Unresolved anger toward others manifests itself in anger toward ourselves that results in depression. In that state of depression, we drag others down with us. Have you ever found yourself in these circumstances? Many have.

10. Lots of fear

The final symptom of unforgiveness in our lives is fear. We live in a world of fear, afraid of our own behaviours and attitudes, afraid of others rejecting us, afraid of our circumstances, and afraid of God. Deep inside, we live with fear that we will one day experience God's anger for what we deserve. In short, we miss the abundant life of a person who is fully pardoned. We continue to live in a prison of 'unforgiven debt'.

The spirit of receiving forgiveness

Now let me show you another scripture which contrasts the spirit of unforgiveness with the spirit of forgiveness. It is found in Luke 7:36–50:

> *Now one of the Pharisees invited Jesus to have dinner with him, so he went to the Pharisee's house and reclined at the table. When a woman who had lived a sinful life in that town learned that Jesus was eating at the Pharisee's house, she brought an alabaster jar of perfume, and as she stood behind him at his feet weeping, she began to wet his feet with her tears. Then she wiped them with her hair, kissed them and poured perfume on them.*
> *When the Pharisee who had invited him saw this, he*

said to himself, 'If this man were a prophet, he would know who is touching him and what kind of woman she is – that she is a sinner.'

Jesus answered him, 'Simon, I have something to tell you.'

'Tell me, teacher,' he said.

'Two men owed money to a certain moneylender. One owed him five hundred denarii, and the other fifty. Neither of them had the money to pay him back, so he cancelled the debts of both. Now which of them will love him more?'

Simon replied, 'I suppose the one who had the bigger debt cancelled.'

'You have judged correctly,' Jesus said.

Then he turned toward the woman and said to Simon, 'Do you see this woman? I came into your house. You did not give me any water for my feet, but she wet my feet with her tears and wiped them with her hair. You did not give me a kiss, but this woman, from the time I entered, has not stopped kissing my feet. You did not put oil on my head, but she has poured perfume on my feet. Therefore, I tell you, her many sins have been forgiven – for she loved much. But he who has been forgiven little loves little.'

Then Jesus said to her, 'Your sins are forgiven.'

The other guests began to say among themselves, 'Who is this who even forgives sins?'

Jesus said to the woman, 'Your faith has saved you; go in peace.'

Here we have a woman with a history. She was probably well known around town as a prostitute. How do we know? For one thing, her unbound hair was a 'give-away'. Secondly, the New American Standard Bible text says,

'And behold, there was a woman in the city who was a sinner'. In the Gospels, this term 'sinner' specifically refers to prostitutes and tax-collectors. So, this woman rather brazenly came into Simon the Pharisee's house to see Jesus while he was at lunch. She had some nerve, entering a religious Pharisee's house! But also she had a deep level of desperation. She knew, without question, that she was a sinner and that she could never repay her debt of sin. But she brought a gift of priceless perfume and gifts of brokenness and tears – the key to her receiving forgiveness. Let's look at what receiving forgiveness involves:

1. Brokenness

She was weeping. She was deeply aware of her sin. No one had to convince her of her sin. No one can produce a spirit of brokenness in us; only the Holy Spirit can release brokenness in our hearts. But we can pray for God to break our hard, proud hearts. We can ask God for circumstances in which our hearts and wills are broken within us. We can ask God for receptivity to the Holy Spirit's work, convicting us of sin, of righteousness and of the judgment to come (John 16:8–11).

2. Humility

In her brokenness, she wet Jesus' feet with her tears, wiping them with her unbound hair. Then, she kissed his feet, pouring perfume on them. She performed as a lowly household servant, but she did it in worship and compassion, not duty. She was not ashamed to be openly humble because she knew this 'man' would give her forgiveness and freedom. She probably had been watching Jesus teaching, healing, doing miracles and confronting the Pharisees. Something inside told her this 'man' would not reject her because of her sin and shame. She wanted freedom and forgiveness more than her pride and dignity. Humility opened the door for her to receive forgiveness.

3. A spirit of worship

Jesus saw this woman's acts of kindness and compassion as acts of faith and worship. Her humility and brokenness were acts of love and worship to Jesus, the Son of God. In common courtesy, Simon the Pharisee should have cared for Jesus' physical needs when he came into his house. But Simon was so self-focused and full of judgment, he did not know how to love and serve his guests. Yet out of her brokenness and humility, this prostitute loved Jesus and humbly worshipped him, regardless of what others thought. Anyone who focuses his attention on Jesus and sees who he really is, also will see himself properly. Focusing on Jesus will naturally lead to a heart seeking forgiveness.

4. She received her forgiveness

Jesus tells Simon the Pharisee in verse 47 that because this woman displayed her love for Jesus, 'her many sins have been forgiven'. This woman's brokenness, humility and loving worship of Jesus opened her heart to receive forgiveness. The Holy Spirit enables us to see our hearts. He produces brokenness in us, releasing humility in our hearts. But we must choose whether to respond in love and worship. When we choose to love Jesus in response to the Holy Spirit's work of conviction, our sins will be removed. If we think, like Simon the Pharisee, that we already have our life straight, we will fail to receive forgiveness from Jesus. This woman heard the message clearly – 'Your sins are forgiven' – and she received forgiveness.

5. Her faith gave her peace

Responding to the sceptics who questioned his authority to forgive sins, Jesus simply turned to this penitent woman and said, 'Your faith has saved you; go in peace.' They not only questioned Jesus' authority but also his authority to pardon someone as bad as this woman. Jesus ignored the questioners. He simply told the woman, 'Your faith, your belief in my word, your response of faith in who I am, has saved you. Go in the peace of your forgiveness.' There is no greater peace than knowing we are forgiven. Those who thought they didn't need forgiveness failed to receive it. This woman, who knew without question that she needed forgiveness, received the most precious gift a person can have.

Jesus told Simon the Pharisee that the person with the bigger debt cancelled would love his master more. But it was not so in the case of the servant forgiven millions in Matthew 18. Why not? Because he approached the king with the attitude that he would pay his debt, rather than humbly receiving his forgiveness. Unlike the prostitute, who knew deeply that she could never repay it, he thought somehow he could. His pride in his own attempt at saving himself hindered him from receiving God's gift of forgiveness. Sometimes we think we have committed sins too bad or too often for God's forgiveness – so we strive to do better rather than turning to Jesus for forgiveness. This is a subtle form of pride. We believe our sin is greater than God's mercy and grace.

If we consistently experience these symptoms of unforgiveness, we need to return to the basics of receiving forgiveness from Father God. We need a fresh touch of his mercy each day. We also need the power of God's grace to live in obedience to him.

Chapter 23

Unforgiveness and Low-grade Anger

Over thirty-four years of marriage, Sherry and I have dealt with many issues of hurt, anger and unforgiveness. I have found these issues to be common in most other marriages. Many married couples think they are living in the freedom of forgiveness. What deceives most couples in this regard, is when little irritants in a marriage are ignored. Just because anger issues leave our conscious memories, doesn't mean they are gone. Many hurts are stored in our hearts and minds and tend to grow in time. Unfortunately, they come back to haunt us years later.

Anger can get stored in us over the course of years, even though we are not aware of its immediate consequence. We harbour unforgiveness because we have not truly forgiven those who offended us. We may think we forgave our spouse, because we have said, 'I forgive you.' But the anger remains and forgiveness does not take hold. The result is, we make numerous unconscious or silent 'vows' not to discuss 'that topic' again. These 'silent vows' then direct our behaviour, unconsciously. It would seem that these vows protect us from getting hurt again, but they don't. We continue to get hurt repeatedly because these vows are actually judgments that we have formed in our minds. Scripture says, 'in the same way you judge others, you will be judged' (Matthew 7:1–2), and thus 'a man reaps what he sows' (Galatians 6:7).

When we do not see our part in the conflict, we judge the other person with the entire fault; we shift all the blame to him or her. When we are hurt and do not forgive, we become a victim of the other person. We feel justified in living in the self-pity of a victim. By shifting the blame and making excuses for our own behaviour, we stop God from searching our hearts for our own issues in the conflict.

The only way out of this endless cycle is to pray, to ask the Holy Spirit to show us our hearts at the cross. At the cross we see Jesus, the perfect Son of God, bearing our sin, rejected by his Father because of us. At the cross, we see we are desperately self-centred, sinful and in need of daily cleansing. God doesn't forgive excuses, he only forgives sins, so we cannot be healed without coming face to face with our own sin that sent Jesus to the cross. James says that we need to grieve, mourn and weep over our sin. Our wrong responses to our hurts and injustices are as sinful as the hurt inflicted by the other person. Until we have a clear revelation of our own sin, confess it, and repent, we will continue to blame-shift. We make excuses for our behaviour, and exist in a state of low-grade anger. In owning our own sin, repenting of our self-will, self-centredness and unforgiveness, we can become free from the tyranny of Satan's trap. In James 5:16 we are told to confess our sins to one another, and we will be healed. Confession and repentance are more than a theological concept. They both must be part of our daily experience.

Learning how to ask for forgiveness

Forgiveness has two sides, like a coin. In this book we have been concentrating primarily on side one. Side one is the hurt you have received from others, which requires your forgiveness. Wherever others have hurt you, you must work through your anger, extending forgiveness to the other person so that you are free from bitterness. However, side two is you hurting others. In this case, you need to seek their forgiveness. When you have wronged others, you must ask forgiveness in the area where you have wronged them. This second aspect of forgiveness is what we are discussing here. Jesus said in Matthew 5:23–26:

> *If you are offering your gift at the altar and there remember that your brother has something against you, leave your gift there in front of the altar. First go and be reconciled to your brother, then come and offer your gift. Settle matters quickly with your adversary who is taking you to court. Do it while you are still with him on the way, or he may hand you over to the judge, and the judge may hand you over to the officer, and you may be thrown into prison. I tell you the truth, you will not get out until you have paid the last penny.*

Getting ready to forgive

None of us easily admits that we have wronged another person. So God gave us the 'signal' of guilt to help us recognize where we have wronged others. Perhaps you, like many people, have learned over time to ignore this 'feeling' or 'signal' of guilt. You do not always recognize the Holy Spirit trying to alert you to something that needs correction in your life or in a relationship. However, as Jesus warned in Matthew 5, failure to care for our side of the offence in a conflict is highly dangerous. When we do not attend to sin in our lives, we become vulnerable to the enemy's attack in that area.

Three steps to seeking forgiveness

Step 1: Acknowledge the need for change

An unforgiving, bitter spirit will prevent a person from experiencing life as God intended. If you do not like your situation, then realize that only you have the power to change it, by allowing the Holy Spirit to work in your heart. When you seek forgiveness for your wrong or for your side of the conflict, you will take a major step towards freedom and emotional health. As you acknowledge your need for change, you will free yourself from the power of the past and the power the other person has over you.

Step 2: Admitting wrong

Step 2 means, specifically, owning responsibility for the wrong you have done. This step is difficult for everybody. Some people acknowledge their wrong only with words, but not with true intentions for change. Accepting responsibility for your wrongs is the basis for changing your behaviour – a crucial step toward forgiveness. When you honestly acknowledge wrong, you are ready for real changes in your own life.

Step 3: Asking forgiveness

In a relationship where two people are hurting, someone must take the initiative to seek forgiveness. Although it is often seen as an admission of weakness, in fact, seeking forgiveness demonstrates strength. A simple statement is all that is necessary. For example: 'I'm sorry for the way I treated you. I was wrong in… [attitude, behaviour or words]. Would you please forgive me?' Usually the answer is 'yes'. If not, or if you doubt the validity of the 'yes', then leave the situation alone. Under no circumstances should you make the other person feel guilty. Conviction is the work of the Holy Spirit. False guilt does nothing to restore a relationship. After seeking forgiveness, you are free in your actions and attitudes toward the other person, even if reconciliation has not yet occurred or never occurs.

Conclusion

Throughout the book, I have stressed the importance of understanding what anger is, how it functions in our body, soul and spirit, and how we can manage it effectively, as a gift from God. I also focused on the power of forgiveness for overcoming the stored anger in our hearts. As stated earlier, all change in us begins with revelation or understanding. You cannot move ahead in spiritual or personal growth if you lack understanding. However, revelation is only the first step. Once you have knowledge of something, you must act on it. Having read this book, you now have greater awareness of anger and forgiveness than you had before. What are you going to do with this knowledge?

Allow me to make some practical suggestions. Begin with prayer, asking the Holy Spirit to guide and direct your next step. If you have discovered substantial buried anger through reading *Healing Life's Hurts*, I would suggest that you need to find a mature and reliable Christian to help you work through your buried anger. Use the Forgiveness Exercise (Appendix 3). With the help of your spiritual companion, release your hurts and buried anger. Then, when you have completed this process, allow the Holy Spirit to direct you into dealing with areas of unresolved guilt or shame from your past. Confess, repent and begin a new pattern of obedience in any areas the Spirit of God shows to you.

If you want to continue growing in Christ, then ask the Holy Spirit to direct you to a man or woman of God who can disciple you into a Godly life. I would not be where I am today in my Christian walk without a faithful man of God, my dear friend Duane Harder, loving, confronting and challenging me. And, an even greater friend to me is my wonderful wife, Sherry. Her willingness to love me despite my weaknesses, yet confront me many times, has been the greatest blessing to me in developing maturity. Cleaning out issues of the past is only the first step in maturing in Christ. Jesus told his disciples in Matthew 28:19–20, when he left the earth, that they were to make disciples of all nations. We often misread that verse and think it says, 'make believers of all nations'. Believers only become disciples when they are discipled. Disciples are learners of Jesus. We only become a disciple if we are discipled by someone more mature in Christ than we are.

May you find such wonderful freedom in Christ through forgiveness and cleansing that your heart for God consumes you in everything you are and do in life. Amen.

Appendix 1

The Components of Aggressive Driving

Below is a test-yourself inventory used for drivers who volunteer to try to change their driving style. By reading the items and how they are organized and scored, you can identify the specific elements that constitute aggressive driving. The following twenty items are arranged along a continuum of escalating degrees of hostility experienced by drivers, beginning with relatively mild forms of aggressiveness (Step 1) and going all the way to ultimate violence (Step 20). How far down the uncivilized road do you sometimes allow yourself to go behind the wheel? The majority of drivers tested go as far as Step 13. How about you?

Test yourself

1. Mentally condemning other drivers.
2. Verbally denigrating other drivers to a passenger in your vehicle.
3. Closing ranks to deny someone entering your lane because you're frustrated or upset.
4. Giving another driver the 'stink eye' to show your disapproval.
5. Speeding past another car or revving the engine as a sign of protest.
6. Preventing another driver from passing because you're mad.

7. Tailgating to pressure a driver to go faster or get out of the way.

8. Fantasizing physical violence against another driver.

9. Honking or yelling at someone through the window to indicate displeasure.

10. Making a visible obscene gesture at another driver.

11. Using your car to retaliate by making sudden, threatening manoeuvres.

12. Pursuing another car in chase because of a provocation or insult.

13. Getting out of the car and engaging in a verbal dispute, on a street or parking lot.

14. Carrying a weapon in the car in case you decide to use it in a driving incident.

15. Deliberately bumping or ramming another car in anger.

16. Trying to run another car off the road to punish the driver.

17. Getting out of the car and beating or battering someone as a result of a road exchange.

18. Trying to run someone down whose actions angered you.

19. Shooting at another car.

20. Killing someone.

Five zones of aggressiveness

1. *The Unfriendly Zone:* Items 1 to 3 – mental and verbal acts of unkindness towards other drivers.

2. *The Hostile Zone:* Items 4 to 7 – visibly communicating

one's displeasure with the desire to punish.

3. *The Violent Zone:* Items 8 to 11 – carrying out an act of hostility, either in fantasy or deed.

4. *The Lesser Mayhem Zone:* Items 12 to 16 – epic road rage contained within one's personal limits.

5. *The Major Mayhem Zone:* Items 17 to 20 – uncontained epic road rage, the stuff of newspaper stories.

© *Leon James, Professor of Psychology, University of Hawaii*

I am grateful to Professor James for permission to reproduce this outline.

Appendix 2

How Was Anger Handled in Your Family?

Your family's view of anger will affect your current view of anger. For example, if your parents expressed their anger through rage, you may do the same thing, or you may try to avoid rage expression at all costs.

- How did your father generally express his anger (e.g. withdrawing, hitting, yelling, moodiness, slapping people)?

- How did your mother generally express her anger (e.g. withdrawal, controlling, yelling, depression, sarcasm, criticizing)?

- When you were a child, how did you generally express your anger (e.g. hitting siblings, talking back, temper tantrums, hiding, crying)?

- How did your parents usually respond to your expressions of anger (e.g. spanking me, yelling at me, putting me in my room)?

- As an adult, I now believe that anger... (e.g. is bad to express, makes me feel guilty, makes things worse, should be avoided)

- My parents generally expressed anger by:

- So now I often express anger by:

- Now, when someone expresses their anger to me, I usually:

- What do you think might happen to you if you allowed yourself to acknowledge that you express anger more often than you thought you did?

- Tick the statements below that apply to your experience of family:

❑ 1. Anger expression (rage) was not acceptable.

❑ 2. Anger expression (rage) was only allowed by the adults in the family.

❑ 3. Anger expression usually involved a lot of yelling.

❑ 4. Anger expression usually involved yelling and then emotional withdrawal.

❑ 5. Any anger expression was seen in the family as a sign of weakness.

❑ 6. We were made to feel ashamed when we expressed anger.

❑ 7. Anger expression often involved violence, throwing things and destruction.

❑ 8. Anger usually resulted in a lecture or bawling out, but nothing more.

❑ 9. Anger was often expressed in our family by someone going into a depression.

❑ 10. We seemed to have a lot of sickness in our home when people were expressing anger.

- Replay the last week in your mind, and see if you can recall at least five things that made your 'anger button' go off.

1. _____

2. _____

3. _____

4. _____

5. _____

- Is it hard for you to recall when your 'anger button' goes off?   Yes ❑   No ❑

Appendix 3

A Forgiveness Exercise

Step 1: List the people you need to forgive

For example: father, mother, brother/sister, boss, spouse, etc.

Step 2: Recognize that bitterness is self-destructive

If you bury negative feelings you have toward others and yourself, you will engage in self-destructive behaviour.

List the ways in which you are now hurting yourself because of the buried anger within you (e.g. overeating or undereating, overdoing exercise, abusing alcohol or drugs, putting yourself down, withdrawing from relationships).

Step 3: Describe briefly what happened

Deal with one person at a time as you go through Steps 3 to 6 – e.g. start with your father and complete him before going on to your mother.)

- It may be specific things said or done to you.

- It may be a specific event that happened to you.
- It may be a general attitude that this person had toward you.
- It may be things that this person failed to do for you.